12-18-88

Dick,

It hardly seems possible another season is gone. This was a great one — New England was just fantastic. As always, I look forward to a new year and a new sailing season. Thanks for the wonderful times.

Happy Holidays,
Bob

THE OYSTER WARS OF CHESAPEAKE BAY

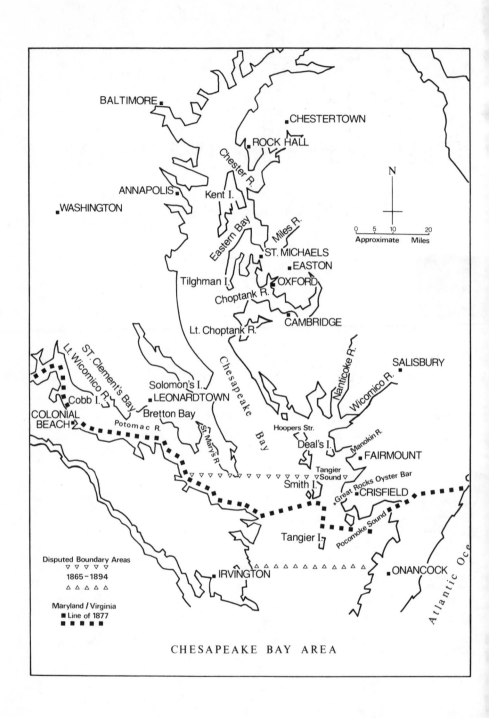

CHESAPEAKE BAY AREA

THE OYSTER WARS OF CHESAPEAKE BAY

John R. Wennersten

TIDEWATER PUBLISHERS

Centreville, Maryland

Library of Congress Cataloging in Publication Data

Wennersten, John R., 1941–
    The oyster wars of Chesapeake Bay.

    Bibliography: p.
    Includes index.
    1. Oyster fisheries—Chesapeake Bay—History.
2. Chesapeake Bay—History. 3. Maryland—Boundaries—
Virginia. 4. Virginia—Boundaries—Maryland. I. Title.
SH365.C4W46   975.5'1804   81-5810
ISBN 0-87033-263-5   AACR2

Manufactured in the United States of America

First edition, 1981; Second printing, 1982

"We have wasted our inheritance by improvidence and mismanagement and blind confidence."

Professor William K. Brooks
Johns Hopkins University, 1892

"If I was a young man looking for a way to earn my living, I'd run as far away from the water as I could."

Captain Orville Parks, 1958

Preacher: "Are you afraid, boy, of dying and going to Hell?"
Waterman: "Naw, Reverend, them drudgers tore that place down long ago."

Dorchester County Folklore

CONTENTS

	List of Illustrations	ix
	Acknowledgments	xi
Prologue:	Follow the Water	3
Chapter One:	Flush Times on the Chesapeake	13
Two:	Hunter Davidson and the Oyster Police	37
Three:	Paddies and Water Arabs	55
Four:	Hell on the Half-Shell	71
Five:	Hard Times	88
Six:	Gunfire on the Potomac	106
Epilogue:	The Vanishing Oystermen	128
Appendix I:	The Maryland Oyster Navy—1891 Joseph B. Seth, Commander	136
Appendix II:	Output of Maryland Oysters, 1839-1910	137
	Bibliography	138
	Index	143

LIST OF ILLUSTRATIONS

Nineteenth century oyster advertisements.	15
John W. Crisfield	19
Women packing and canning oysters at Crisfield, Maryland	24
Baltimore oyster peddler	29
Eating oysters on the dock	31
Dredgers at the hand windlass	34
Black watermen	40
Police pursue oyster pirates	44
Pirates dredging at night	44
A cruel winter for tongers	57
Pirates attack the *Julia Hamilton*	75
The capture of a pirate	75
Police steamer *McLane*	81
Police steamer *Venus*	81
Black women canning oysters	91
Potomac River oyster police, *Pocomoke* and others	110
The vanishing skipjack	131
The vanishing watermen	132

ACKNOWLEDGMENTS

I FIRST BECAME interested in the story of the Chesapeake oyster wars in 1976, when I was involved in a number of bicentennial projects for the state of Maryland. My original curiosity soon gave way to fascination as I learned about the adventures of the oyster pirates and the centuries-long dispute between Maryland and Virginia over the Potomac River and the Chesapeake Bay boundary.

The general expansion of urban culture on the Atlantic seaboard has overwhelmed many maritime communities, and the distinctive life of the Chesapeake watermen will soon vanish. Thus it was my purpose to chronicle the great nineteenth- and twentieth-century oyster conflicts before the passage of time eroded available records and while the story still remained in the main current of the Chesapeake's oral tradition.

During this book's progress many people have given generously of their time and expertise. Mr. Orlando Wootten deserves special thanks. His skill as a photographer and an historian made my task much easier than it would otherwise have been. Mr. Alex Kellam, who is a veritable storehouse of Chesapeake lore, furnished me with many insights on the travail of oystermen after the turn of the century. The late Governor Millard Tawes granted me many interviews, a number of which focused on the oyster industry and Maryland's historic quarrel with Virginia. Mr. Landon Curley and Captain Ellsworth Hoffman were especially helpful in providing me with insights on the Potomac River war of the 1950s.

ACKNOWLEDGMENTS

I would especially like to express my gratitude to the Wye Institute for a general research grant in Eastern Shore studies. Several years ago, Jim Nelson, the director of the institute, told me that the culture and heritage of the Eastern Shore of Maryland was rich enough to provide many a writer with his life's work. As time goes on I am learning how right that observation was.

Mr. Kenneth Kahn and Mr. James Burgess of the Maryland Arts Council have strongly supported my literary endeavors. In an era of diminishing financial support of the arts, the Maryland Arts Council has vigorously defended state programs for regional artists and writers.

Lastly, I owe a special debt to Ruth Ellen, Stewart, and Matthew, who always remind me what is important in life.

THE OYSTER WARS OF CHESAPEAKE BAY

Prologue

FOLLOW THE WATER

FEW DENIZENS of the ocean's depths have enjoyed as interesting a social history as the oyster. A sedentary bivalve found clustered in the bottoms of bays and river outlets to the sea, the oyster has been relentlessly pursued by man since prehistoric times. Our first indication of man's interest in oysters comes from the presence of their shells, often in enormous numbers, in prehistoric kitchen middens in various coastal areas of the world. Archaeologists have discovered evidences of an oyster industry at Neanderthal sites at Gilbraltar and in Portugal; and large oyster shell mounds have also been discovered in Japan and Australia and Kattegat in Denmark, though oysters no longer flourish there because of the lowered salinity of the water. In the Mediterranean, the great German archaeologist Schliemann found heaps of oyster shells in his excavations at Mycenae in southern Greece.

Oysters occupied a place of honor in ancient Rome, and thousands of them were consumed at feasts and festivals by the aristocracy. Juvenal, the satirist of imperial Rome, wrote of lavish nightly banquets and beautiful women "who at deep midnight on fat oysters sup." Many Roman aristocrats had such insatiable appetites that when feasting they would occasionally leave the room to relieve their stomachs by artificial means and then return to a fresh supply of oysters. This custom was universal throughout the empire, and Roman matrons carried peacock feathers and other throat-ticklers for that purpose.

3

THE OYSTER WARS

Oysters were so highly prized by the Romans that they dispatched their slaves to the seacoast of the Atlantic to gather them for feasts; many Roman houses contained great tanks of water in which oysters were kept fresh for the table. During the Roman occupation of Britain in 78 B.C., oysters were exported at great expense and with much difficulty from the Kentish coast to Italy. The oysters were carried in bags tightly packed with snow and ice to prevent the opening of the shells and the loss of moisture necessary to keep them alive. The Romans also had considerable dredging operations at the sight of modern Yarmouth. As Rome's navy ransacked the English coast in search of the tasty bivalve, the poet Sallust exclaimed, "Poor Britons—there is some good in them after all. They produce an oyster!"

Their love of oysters prompted the Romans to experiment with aquaculture. Pliny the Elder in his *Natural History* writes of one Sergius Orata who at the time of Christ experimented with artificial oyster beds at Baiae to enlarge his income. The Roman writer Ausonius in the fourth century A.D. described how oysters were brought from Brindisium to Lago Lucrino north of Naples. A small lake was connected by a narrow channel to the Mediterranean. Here oysters were twisted into loosely woven ropes and then suspended in salt water by stakes driven into the bottom of the lake. Thus oysters could be grown over soft bottoms on which they could not otherwise live. The Romans also found a variety of uses for oyster shells. They reduced them to powder to cure wounds and ulcers, rashes on infants, and to clean their teeth. Powdered oyster shells were also used to repair tile baths and as a cement in high-quality construction.

During the Dark Ages, the popularity of oysters declined until 1066, when the conquering Normans revived the oyster trade in England. By 1189, towns along the Kentish and Essex coasts had received charters from the king of England to collect and sell oysters. Throughout the centuries that followed, Englishmen exploited the vast oyster beds that lay off the mouth of the Thames, along the north coast of Kent. By 1557 these beds were in danger of extinction, and the British government prohibited dredging in the Thames estuary. These first attempts at conservation, however, only intensified the public appetite; and in London oystermongers sold millions of Colchester and Whitstable oysters annually at four to the penny. When the East India Company met in London at Merchant Tailor's Hall for its annual banquet in 1662, the menu included roast mutton with oysters followed by broiled oysters, oyster pie, and pickled oysters.

The Chesapeake Bay has provided the oyster with an exceptional domain covering 2,300 square miles. It is relatively free of the starfish and oyster drills that prey on oyster beds, and the hospitable temperatures and less saline waters of the Chesapeake guarantee a bountiful spatfall. Wonderously reproductive, female oysters release millions of eggs, and males produce a comparable amount of sperm. After six or seven days the fertilized larva acquires a shell, thereby becoming known as "spat," and settles back to the bottom where it attaches itself to the oyster bed, or cultch. The oyster beds of the Chesapeake are usually found in water less than forty feet deep. Few are found in the great channel that runs the length of the Bay—the bottom is too soft and muddy for oysters. The largest beds are found in the small bays, creeks, and river mouths of the Chesapeake in water that varies in depth from two to thirty feet.

When Captain John Smith visited the Chesapeake shore of North America in the seventeenth century, he observed that the Indians were well acquainted with oysters and valued them highly. The Nanticoke Indians, for example, were fond of raking up large piles of fresh oysters from creek bottoms with forked sticks and indulging in feasts that sometimes lasted several days. The largest oyster midden left by the Indians in the Chesapeake Bay region covered nearly thirty acres of land near Pope's Creek on the Potomac River. Similarly, history records a mound containing eight million cubic feet of oyster shells near an Indian village on the Damariscotta River in the state of Maine. British colonists first tasted Chesapeake oysters in 1607. While at Cape Henry, Captain John Smith and his men discovered an Indian campfire in a wood clearing and found several baskets heaped high with oysters. They ate some raw and roasted others, and Captain Smith found them "large and delicate in taste." Oysters were so plentiful in the Bay during this period that occasionally ships would run aground on oyster beds like the huge "oyster reef" at the mouth of King's Creek on the Virginia shore.

The first settlers in the region identified Chesapeake oysters as a hardship food. Colonists on Kent Island, for example, often complained during economic and political crises in the Bay country that they were "reduced to eating oysters." Also, during the starving time in Jamestown, a number of colonists repaired to the oyster banks of the lower James River and subsisted for nine weeks on nothing but oysters and a pint of Indian corn apiece per week.

All that was needed to harvest Chesapeake oysters, wrote an English visitor in 1702, was a boat and a pair of wooden tongs—wide at the end and tipped with iron. The colonists pinched the tongs together and pulled up clumps of oysters from the Bay bottom. In 1705, Francis Makemie, the famous Presbyterian preacher, encouraged colonists to exploit the Chesapeake's resources and formulated an elaborate plan for transoceanic trade in pickled oysters. Unfortunately his dream of turning the Chesapeake into a seafood empire was not realized during the colonial period.

Throughout the pre-Revolutionary period colonists invested heavily in land and slaves as the booming tobacco industry dictated that the Bay country would be an empire founded upon smoke. Soaring land prices and the unpredictability of the tobacco staple forced many poor whites to seek their livelihood from the Chesapeake by working in shipyards like those at Chestertown and Oxford, or by catching herring and oysters which merchants and planters exported in large amounts to Jamaica and London. In the 1760s George Washington operated a thriving seafood business at his Mount Vernon landing, and the fastidious colonel occasionally had difficulties with feisty and foul-mouthed oystermen.

By the outbreak of the Revolution the increase in population and the growing prosperity of the eastern seaboard contributed to the growth of professional fisheries. Oysters, once hardship's food, grew in popularity. By 1779 advertisements for oyster sellers in Maryland, New York, and Massachusetts were widely circulated from Boston to Williamsburg. In Maryland, farmers spread oysters on their fields as manure and used them in local smelters for making iron.

Visitors to the Chesapeake whose ships occasionally stopped at waterfront communities were surprised by the local squalor and described the watermen as "coarse and slatternly people who live in small log huts of one or two rooms and subsist on salt meat, oysters, and crude bread." Most of these folk owned a small boat or log canoe, a cooking pot, and a few tools. For recreation they turned to storytelling, fighting, and hard drink. Liquor tempered the harshness of Chesapeake life, and in the taverns and ordinaries of the Bay country both men and women could get "drunk for a penny and dead drunk for two pence." Dissenting religious beliefs like Quakerism and Presbyterianism were also popular with these people, who disliked the pretensions of the Anglican squirearchy. Anglican missionaries received a cool reception in waterfront communities and in turn were exasperated by these "half-savage and nearly pagan people." In the Chesapeake, human life was cheap, and watermen followed a code of justice enforced by knife and gun. Long after the Bay country had come under the domination of haughty self-made tobacco nabobs and lawyers, the small communities on the islands, creeks, and necks of the Chesapeake would retain their frontier character.

The colonial Chesapeake was a harsh environment. "We are swarming with Bugs, Musquetoes, worms of every sort,"

Henry Callister complained in his travels in the Bay country in 1750. The Eastern Shore of Maryland, he wrote, was a vast swamp full of "Spiders, Snakes, Hornets, Wasps, sea nettles, ticks, gnats, thunder and lightning—excessive heat, excessive cold." Hurricanes and malaria-bearing swamp mosquitoes decimated island and riverfront communities. Harsh winters locked the Bay in an icy grip, and often it was not until late March that ships could navigate the Chesapeake. Women in these waterfront communities married before the age of sixteen and were quickly exhausted from excessive childbearing. Most were toothless and haggard at the age of twenty-five. Chesapeake men, wrote many observers, tended to be "blasphemous, quarrelsome, and licentious." Maimed and scarred from timber cutting and life on the water as sailors and fishermen, they acquired a grizzled appearance from exposure to the weather.

During the American Revolution, Chesapeake watermen rallied to the British side because of their hatred for Maryland's slave-holding rebel gentry. Many poor watermen had been humiliated by arrogant planters who chose to treat them worse than slaves, and throughout the war there were numerous revolts against the revolutionary government in the seaside villages of the Bay country. Often Tory watermen served as brokers of trade with British warships and made handsome profits. Others turned to piracy and looted American ships on the Bay. Of the Tory watermen on the Chesapeake at this time, none was more infamous than Joe Whaland. Throughout the Revolution he commanded a heavily armed crew of eight whites and twenty-seven blacks which raided the Chesapeake shore. In December 1780, Whaland's pirate galley appeared in the Wicomico River, and local revolutionaries informed Annapolis that "Joseph Whaland, that old offender, is down in Somerset plundering again." Whaland was a tall, wiry, grim-looking fellow who wore fancy linen shirts and a gold-embroidered waistcoat. He knew the Bay well and was especially familiar with the channels of Dorchester and Somerset county waterways. Although he was captured four times by the militia, he seldom remained in custody for long. Pirate gangs, wrote Maryland Attorney General Luther Martin, committed such acts of "villainy" that the patriot cause on the lower Eastern Shore was imperiled.

On the upper Eastern Shore the notorious "China" Clows raided bayside plantations in Queen Anne's County and liberated slaves. Captured in his home on Kent Island after a fierce gun fight, Clows was hanged by the Maryland militia in 1788. Thus during the revolutionary conflict, Tory watermen caused such havoc on the Eastern Shore that an army of occupation frequently had to be stationed in the Bay country. These watermen, in the words of one frustrated American militia commander were "a set of Poor, Ignorant, Illitorate People. Yet they are Artful and Cunning as Foxes."

The Revolutionary War on the waters of the Chesapeake seriously disrupted the fishing and oyster industries of Maryland's Eastern Shore. The lack of salt prevented watermen from curing shad and herring, and British depredations along the Atlantic coast curtailed Maryland's oyster commerce with New York and Philadelphia. The Revolution, however, did have one positive effect on the Chesapeake economy. The increased military significance of the region reinforced the need for accurate charts of Chesapeake Bay, which were a boon to Maryland watermen. By the war's end, Chesapeake mariners could rely upon charts which provided depth soundings for the Chester, Miles, and Choptank rivers and for Tangier and Pocomoke sounds as well.

In the years that followed the Revolution, it was Methodism rather than the ideology of the new republic that tamed many of the Chesapeake's wild and rebellious watermen. When the first Methodist preachers arrived in the 1790s to preach on Tangier and Deal's islands, they were met with great hostility. According to Adam Wallace, a Methodist preacher of that era, the watermen first believed that the Methodists were "nothing but a parcel of Irishmen who have run away from their own country to keep from being hanged." Said one waterman of the period: "The Methodists have great larning, and know no other way to get along but going about raising the devil by their preaching and carrying on, and make the people worship them and give them money." Methodist preachers, however, were not to be underestimated. At church and revival services they could use their fists, and often gave the Methodist gospel with blood running down their faces. Also the Methodists soon won the confidence of the poorly schooled watermen because they were people who "could pray without a book or preach without a sermon written out, or exhort with words unstudied."

The most notable Methodist success in the islands of the Chesapeake was the conversion of Joshua Thomas in 1807. A rough, awkward, stammering islander, Joshua Thomas spread the gospel throughout the Chesapeake in his big log canoe named, appropriately, *Methodist*. In his sermons and discourses at the first camp meeting on Tangier Island in 1809, Thomas drew his illustrations from fishing, oystering, and sailing—pursuits in which he had spent most of his life. Thomas knew the watermen and their hopes and fears, and his rough sermons usually overcame the pagan resistance of people who lived on drum fish, sweet potatoes, and oysters. When the British occupied Tangier Island during the War of 1812, Thomas preached to the troops and became a legend in the region for his prediction that the British would not take Baltimore.

In August 1828, Joshua Thomas preached at the first camp meeting held on Deal's Island. Tents were erected for the services and encampment; and over two hundred sailboats and two steamboats converged on the island. The camp meeting attracted the sick, the weary, and the seekers after Christ's salvation. Unfortunately, it also brought hucksters who set up booths on the beach for hardware, dry goods, and millinery. Some of the watermen and their wives were so busy shopping that they forgot about the preaching. The "abomination of liquor" could not be kept away either, and sometimes drunken oystermen would cause trouble among the order-loving and the religious. As visitors to the region quickly found, not even Methodism could restrain the exhuberant individualism of the watermen. Methodism did, however, mitigate some of the physical and spiritual harshness of Chesapeake life and added a stabilizing element of religiosity to many a waterfront community.

By 1820 the waterfront societies of Chesapeake Bay had reached their maturity and would remain relatively unchanged into the twentieth century. So dependent were the watermen on the resources of the Chesapeake Bay that one visitor from Philadelphia remarked that they could "almost be called an amphibious race; for nearly all the men and boys spend their lives on the water." Their canoes hollowed out of pine logs, were rigged with two masts with sails attached, which could easily be taken down or put up. From infancy the people took to sailing vessels and, he added, "a landsman would be amazed to see one of these small boys out in a gale, perched on the windward side, almost blown out of the water, riding on the rolling billows, and looking as unconcerned as if on his accustomed cricket in the chimney corner." Their log canoes, watermen boasted, could outsail any vessel on the Bay not propelled by steam. Oystermen were easily identified by their homespun clothes—a light striped jacket, pants rolled halfway up to their knees, and a little round hat. Nearly everyone went barefoot; shoes were regarded as superfluous by these hardy and simple people.

Known to the merchants of Baltimore as "oyster catchers," watermen ferried oysters up the Bay to the city and sold them to local packers. In the summer months watermen carried melons, salt fish, and sweet potatoes to Norfolk and Baltimore. When the Civil War erupted in 1861, Maryland's watermen professed loyalty to the Union and enjoyed a thriving illegal commerce with the Confederacy; many schooners based at Deal's Island were employed by Richmond as blockade runners. Although the Union Navy placed gunboats on the Bay to stop smuggling during the conflict, they were no match for the elusive Chesapeake mariners.

These Chesapeake men knew but one vocation in life—to follow the water. Spiritual ancestors of the men of antiquity who had pursued the almighty oyster, the men of the Bay country stood defiantly apart from the agrarian society of the Eastern Shore. In the years after the Civil War they would participate in one of the biggest seafood bonanzas in history, and their exploits would become part of Maryland's history and folklore.

Chapter 1

FLUSH TIMES ON THE CHESAPEAKE

T HROUGHOUT the winter of 1867, seafood packers, commission merchants, and ship captains crowded the large, black-and-white marble lobby of the Maltby House Hotel in Baltimore. The four-storied hotel dominated the harbor and served as the nerve center of the Chesapeake Bay oyster industry. Seafood speculators never strayed too far, because Caleb S. Maltby, the hotel's feisty owner, was also Baltimore's leading oyster broker; contracts were won and oyster prices set on the premises.

On a blustery November morning, Caleb Maltby limped impatiently into his hotel in search of a ship's captain for one of his oyster boats. Despite his seventy years and frail health, Maltby was feared and respected in the industry. Old Maltby, the packers said, thrived on competition and boasted that the oyster business was fang and claw and not much else. Maltby owned three large oyster vessels, and occasionally his fleet cleared from fifteen to seventeen thousand dollars on a single trip to New Haven or Boston. On this day, however, he had no luck finding a captain. The northeast winds were blowing hard, and a heavily laden oyster boat could founder easily in an Atlantic storm.

Arriving from Connecticut in 1836 to open a packing plant and fresh oyster operation in Baltimore, Maltby had been part of a general migration of New England seafood brokers to the Chesapeake. In Long Island Sound, New York and Connecticut watermen had resorted to a device called the *dredge*, a scooplike instrument pulled by rope or cable across an oyster bar by a sailing ship. The dredges left few oysters for reproduction, and the beds of Long Island Sound were quickly exhausted. Similarly, the disappearance of oysters off Cape Cod forced Massachusetts to import large numbers of the tasty bivalve. In his "Cape Cod Essays" Henry David Thoreau remarks that about sixty thousand bushels of Chesapeake oysters were brought by Baltimore clipper ships to Wellfleet in the 1850s. New England dredge boats soon entered Chesapeake Bay, and their reports of abundant seafood brought on a great oyster rush. Northerners and their dredge boats, however, were not welcomed on the Bay. Marylanders protested against the "plundering Yankee drudgers" and passed a law banning oystering by nonresidents. Thus Maltby, Abiathar Field, and other oyster brokers moved to Baltimore to protect their livelihood. They could not have arrived in the Chesapeake at a more opportune time.

The establishment of oyster-packing houses in Baltimore by New England businessmen coincided with the building of the Baltimore and Ohio Railroad, and as train service began to open the hinterland, the oyster packers of Baltimore wasted little time in sending shipments westward. Even before the line was completed, packers sent wagonloads of oysters in the winter season over the Cumberland Road to Pittsburgh, Wheeling, and the Middle West. Once completed, the Baltimore and Ohio Railroad served as a powerful marketing stimulus for the oyster industry, and by 1860 the railroad annually carried over three million pounds of oysters westward. What had originally been a tiny business of the Baltimore docks ballooned into a million-dollar business on the eve of the Civil War; nearly sixty packing houses lined the city wharf.

The Civil War subsequently disrupted the Chesapeake Bay economy. During the conflict Maryland watermen found smuggling and the freight business more profitable than oystering. At the war's end, however, two developments spurred an unprecedented expansion of the oyster industry: the development of a reliable steam-canning process that allowed for long-distance transport of oysters,

Nineteenth century oyster advertisements. Courtesy: Maryland Extension Service.

and a booming postwar economy that gave people additional money to purchase status-conferring comforts and delicacies. In the 1850s a hungry traveller lodging in Pittsburgh in winter considered himself to be among life's fortunate if he could have his oyster stew. During the postwar era, in regions as distant as the silver and gold fields of Colorado and California, miners hungrily consumed large helpings of oysters as a regular staple. By 1870 oysters were selling at 45 cents a bushel and were the vanguard of a fifty-million-dollar seafood industry. Small wonder, then, that the activities of Caleb Maltby and the other oyster brokers were as closely watched by Baltimore businessmen as the New York stock market.

Across the Bay, the Eastern Shore of Maryland was awakened by the oyster boom. Like some tidewater Rip Van Winkle stirred from the sleep of decades, the region after the Civil War throbbed with a new and lively pulse. In the marshes that connected Somers Cove with the drier lands of Somerset County, two hundred Civil War veterans worked feverishly in the April 1867 humidity to complete the final section of track that would connect the bayside village with mile-a-minute rail service to Philadelphia. As the gandy dancers spiked the rails, they cursed the premature arrival of summer and the merciless salt-marsh mosquitoes. On the Eastern Shore, wrote Bayard Taylor, the famous New York traveller, "time is money" was replacing the old notion that "time was made for slaves."

John Crisfield, chief promoter and president of the Eastern Shore Railroad, and his friends had quietly acquired rights of way to Somers Cove. Crisfield knew that the region stood at the threshold of an economic boom in the seafood industry when he and his partner, Michael Somers, first saw that fleet of downeast Yankee oyster boats. Somers Cove stood at the gateway to Tangier Sound, one of the richest oyster grounds in the world, and Crisfield and his partners hoped to make a killing in the railroad construction and land speculation that the boom would foster. When the first surging locomotive came within one mile of the huge wharf that stretched out into the Sound, ox carts carried tons of oysters to the impatiently hissing train. Hundreds of boats tonged for oysters within sight of the railroad depot, and one observer of the transformation that accompanied the railroad's arrival noted that "the oyster houses are rising as if by magic, not only from the marshes, but from the very water where only a few months ago, vessels used to anchor." Years later local folks would say that when John Crisfield slipped from the oyster wharf into the Bay, he baptized the town in his own name.

Crisfield, an overnight seafood mecca, stood on a giant mound of oyster shells glistening white in the sun. By then well connected by rail to the Northeast, Crisfield by 1872 had the largest oyster trade in the state and provided employment for over six hundred sailing vessels. Crisfield sent its oysters throughout the country and to distant ports in Europe and Australia. Along the rickety docks that were once salt marsh, large heaps of oyster shells identified the presence of packing houses and shucking operations. During the 1870s several million bushels of oysters were harvested annually by Crisfield-based boats, and every morning, Sundays excepted, from twenty to thirty railroad cars could be seen moving from the packing houses, heavily freighted with oysters.

Crisfield was a cluttered, muddy town that reverberated to the noise of rolling barrels, steam whistles, shouting boys, and the voices of burly black stevedores. Three steamboats a day pulled into Crisfield, and on the wharf drovers cracked their whips over teams of oxen and yelled "Ai! Ai!, Ho!" to the two-thousand-pound beasts as they pulled loads of oysters, sweet potatoes, and tomatoes to the churning steamboats. Wagons swayed through traffic, splattering mud on the windows of stores and offices in the jerry-built oyster port.

A get-rich-quick spirit prevailed in Crisfield, and the attendant lawlessness of local life made this waterfront community resemble a rough, sprawling mining town of the great western frontier. The lure of the almighty oyster attracted a swelling population of merchants, immigrants, gamblers, bootleggers, and prostitutes. New York dandies with "sea legs" more appropriate for Hudson River excursions scrambled on the Bay in rigs whose unseaworthiness complemented the ignorance of their owners. Those who visited Crisfield in the 1870s found a raw, riotous community with saloons and brothels filled with lusty watermen fresh from their sloops after weeks at a time out on the Bay. To the consternation of the town's polite society, the whores and chorus girls of John Blizzard's burlesque establishment merrily entertained hundreds of watermen. These "painted ladies" had followed the fortunes of the Union Army in Maryland and had worked out West in the Comstock Lode country before coming to Crisfield. During oyster season the large boxing ring in the middle of John Burgess's restaurant and saloon was a crucible of violence. Here Smith Islanders battled Virginia watermen in no-holds-barred conflict. The feud between the Smith Islanders and the Virginians dated back to the colonial period when watermen first began to fight over fishing grounds and oyster beds; the slugfests in the boxing ring were merely a continuation of the violence that was a way of life on Tangier Sound.

In the small, tightly knit community of Smith Island, twelve miles out in the Bay from Crisfield, Haynie Bradshaw was known as a devout Christian and the best friend that a man could ever have. For most of the year Bradshaw was a pillar of the island's Methodist church; often when the island lacked a preacher, he led services and superintended the Sunday school. Occasionally when one of his long-winded friends was too long in the pulpit, Haynie would bellow, "Brother, let's hurry that sermon along to safe anchor!" Haynie liked to read the Bible, and it seemed fitting that this big, raw-boned, muscular man would delight in the story of Samson. The Methodist Church forbade whiskey and beer on the island, and there was little sin to tempt a human soul. Often during church services Haynie would exclaim, "Brothers and sis-

John W. Crisfield. Courtesy: Library of Congress.

ters, I feel this morning like an old bateau after she has been pulled up on her rollers and had her bottom scraped. No more do the barnacles of sin foul my bottom, for I've been washed clean in the blood of the lamb."

It was only during oyster season that Haynie Bradshaw fell from grace. The fierce competition of oystering and the rough winter weather of the Chesapeake whetted his fighting instincts. When aroused, this Christian loved to fight, and during his lapses from the Methodist fold he was known as one of the scrappiest dockside brawlers on the Eastern Shore and the staunchest defender of Smith Island's honor.

Severn Riggin first saw Haynie Bradshaw fight in the autumn of 1875. Haynie had landed his boat at the wharf of Riggin's general store at Crisfield to pick up a barrel of flour. As he was paying the clerk, two Virginia watermen began to taunt him. "Hey, ain't you one o'them dumb Smith Islanders?" jeered one man. Suddenly a fist exploded in his face, dissolving his nose into a bloody pulp. Haynie then lunged towards his partner and flung him into the Bay. Still flushed with anger, Bradshaw grabbed the four-hundred-pound barrel of flour and rolled it over to his bateau as if it were empty.

Later that evening Severn Riggin saw Haynie Bradshaw fight several Virginia watermen in the ring at John Burgess's saloon. The drunken crowd roared with delight at the bare-knuckled combat, and the sawdust around the ring was soon spattered with blood. Finally Haynie's opponents withdrew, and the swollen-eyed defender of Smith Island was carried victoriously to the bar. On some nights the fighting would spill out of the saloon into the muddy street and men would take out their knives. But on this occasion the Virginia watermen had had their fill of the "dumb Smith Islander."

Fistfights and brawls were common in Crisfield and other waterfront towns; the Bay country bred a fierce recklessness in men who pitted their lives against the wild elements of the Chesapeake. Goodsell's Alley, a street lined with businesses and saloons, was a source of constant fighting. The brawling and cursing became so intolerable one night that Thomas Hudson, whose second-floor bedroom opened on the alley, took his shotgun and fired two rounds into the street to disperse the brawlers, so that local residents could get a night's sleep. Crisfield, however, remained neither quiet nor dull as long as Harvey Johnson, a prominent local saloon keeper, served as justice of the peace. Every morning he would rap on the table and announce, "Gentlemen the court is now in session, but I call your attention to the fact that business is still going on at the bar."

To curb drunken lawlessness, the town commissioners voted Crisfield dry on December 8, 1875. Prohibition, however, did little to temper the town's salty rowdies. Oystermen quickly turned to "walking saloons" and speakeasies. The town's original jail, a railroad boxcar, soon proved inadequate, and the city fathers constructed a large log-cabin jail where watermen could nurse their wounds and their hangovers.

The "roaring Crisfielders" would do anything on a bet. In March 1872, the famous Shakespeare Saloon in Washington advertised an oyster-eating contest with fifty dollars in gold awarded to the winner. Crisfield supported Georgie Fields, a red-faced schooner captain, against a German immigrant. During the contest the two men together consumed seven bushels of oysters—forty dozen—raw, fried, and stewed. They spent three hours at the table and expended $7.50 before declaring the contest a draw. Afterwards the German went on an eight-mile hike; the Crisfielder went to bed and fell ill.

In the summertime Crisfield's lusty watermen became the object of Methodist evangelical efforts. Watermen would arrive at camp meetings by wagonloads from the packing houses, saloons, and wharves. The lean horses would be unhooked from their wagons and tied in the shade of trees while their owners flocked to concession stands selling ice cream and candy. At times these religious revivals or "Love Feasts" had a circus atmosphere, with hard drinking and

21

gambling taking place just out of earshot of the pulpit. At camp meetings, watermen laughed, "more souls were begot than saved." On August 16, 1873, a train load of Methodist women from Salisbury arrived in Crisfield to convert the ungodly. The women were dressed in their best finery and paraded through the streets, to the delight of the watermen. Later the town thronged to the twenty-five revival tents that the ladies had established a short distance from Crisfield in Nelson's Woods. Unfortunately, a fierce rain and electrical storm disrupted the proceedings before Crisfield's lost souls could be rescued. To many Methodists it seemed that in Crisfield even nature was leagued against the Holy Writ and the public peace.

Crisfield's industry impressed visitors. "Oysters, oysters, are everywhere, in barrels, in boxes, in cans, in buckets, in the shell and out," declared *Harper's* in 1879. Throughout the town the air was permeated with the tidal odor of mudbanks and "defunct oysters." Passengers on board the steamer *City of Norfolk* beheld a strange sight when the port of Crisfield came into view. To their surprise they saw a shanty town on stilts, a town of poles and myriads of boats of all sizes and descriptions. A town of oysters, built on oyster shells: such was Crisfield, the queen of honky-tonks and mistress of the oyster empire of Tangier Sound.

The same booster spirit and lusty optimism founded upon the oyster treasure of Chesapeake Bay prevailed elsewhere in the region. On the blue waters of the Choptank River, the thriving town of Cambridge sparkled in the sunlight. In 1871 Cambridge's population had grown to two thousand, and the town boasted new frame houses and four hotels. Across a bridged inlet, old homes built of bricks brought from England as ballast reminded visitors of the town's colonial past. Cambridge's citizens and officials were quick to sing the oyster's praise. "It furnishes employment to thousands," declared Robert Wilson in *Lippincott's Magazine*, "and it contributes largely to popular education through oyster license taxes, promotes social intercourse, and keeps the lawyers and physicians in practice when other resources fail."

Oyster optimism prevailed in uneasy juxtaposition to old prejudices. Many of Cambridge's rich seafood packers were parvenu watermen who had gambled on the future and won. In their pursuit of a fast dollar these oystermen worked side by side with blacks and ignored many of the rules of the color bar. Such actions prompted the Dorchester County gentry to complain that in Cambridge "mongrels were usurping the kennels of thoroughbreds." In turn the oyster nabobs displayed their contempt for rigid social codes by asserting that Jim Crowism was a landsman's preoccupation that had no place on Chesapeake Bay. Many watermen vowed that they would "tong oysters with the Devil" if they could make money at it. Such thinking was current in Dorchester even before the Civil War. In 1865 John Stevens, a wealthy ship captain and oyster broker who worked in Cambridge and Easton, built a thirty-thousand-dollar schooner called the *Carrie Stevens*. He presented this floating palace of a boat to the Maryland Colonization Society to be used to transport emancipated slaves to Liberia and to train Negro sailors and pilots.

With the advent of the autumn rains the fog banks would steal up the Chesapeake and fall over the Eastern Shore with a dripping embrace. It was at this time that a waterman's life began to lose its romance. The cold and dampness of the Bay prematurely aged men, and in water-locked hamlets like Oxford the most noticeable characteristics of a waterman were iron-gray hair and a deeply lined brow. In the saloons along Oxford's docks men complained of chest misery; and too many, local doctors knew, had cough-wracked bodies honeycombed with tuberculosis.

Yet the growth of Oxford's oyster-packing industry had pumped life's blood throughout the town's lazy veins. Hundreds of boats fresh from the beds of the Tred Avon River bobbed at the wharf's edge, their masts wrapped in sails and loaded to the gunwales with oysters. During the oyster sea-

Women packing and canning oysters at Crisfield, Maryland,
Harper's Weekly, March 16, 1872.

son Oxford was transformed from a faded old Talbot County waterfront town into a thriving seafood market. Hundreds of Negroes and immigrants arrived by train in the first weeks of the packing season "to work oysters"; to the conservative townspeople these men and women looked like a ragged band of refugees. They came in a variety of dress—from the previous winter's overalls to suits and shirts with high, starchy collars. Their luggage was a fantastic jumble of tattered valises, carpetbags, suitcases, overflowing pillowcases, and huge blanketed bundles tied with rope. Most of the blacks who flocked into Oxford and St. Michaels came from as far south as North Carolina and Virginia; those not arriving by train came by way of Baltimore on the steamers *Olive* and *Samuel J. Pentz.*

Black oyster shuckers were the backbone of the town's seafood economy, and Oxford packers cultivated their good will. Good shuckers were prized, and many of the Negroes who came to Oxford could shuck an oyster in less than five seconds. During the season the barons of the local packing industry sponsored fried-oyster dinners for their black employees. The food and the beer were free, and a small band was hired to play waltzes. Usually a black church hall or a warehouse was decorated in bunting, and hundreds of blacks would feast at the long plank and sawhorse tables. Later, as the band played louder and the men became lager-logged, an argument would erupt, followed by a flashing knife or a pistol shot. The brawling oystermen would be arrested and the waltzes would continue as if nothing had happened.

Oxford's low-raftered oyster houses were smelly, sloppy places that would have nauseated the fancy men and women who relished Chesapeake oysters in the smart restaurants of New York and Philadelphia. Shuckers stood in the narrow body-width stalls at small tables while men went up and down the aisles with flat-bottomed barrows, bringing fresh supplies of oysters to the shuckers and carrying off the shells that had been cast aside. Oyster juice trickled on the floor amid piles of muddy oysters as female shuckers used their knives with great dexterity to obtain the Bay's treasure. A bemused spectator reported the process: "She seizes an oyster, inserts the knife between the shells, then with a quick turn of the wrist, the shell is opened, the oyster cut loose and dropped into the pan, all with one movement." Sometimes a visitor stared at the shucking knife and asked, "Aren't you afraid of cutting your hand?" A black woman looked up from her work and stated flatly that "when you does this season in an' season out, you don't know what cuttin' yo' hand is." The men and women in the stalls frequently stopped to warm their hands which had become numbed from handling cold oysters. Occasionally in winter a welcome ray of sunlight would pierce the gloom of the oyster houses and the shuckers would begin to sing an old dragging spiritual:

> Dere is rest fo' de weary—
> Dere is rest fo' de weary—
> Dere is rest fo' me!
> On de othe side o' Jordon—
> In de green fields o' Eden—
> Where de tree o' life is bloomin—
> Dere is rest fo' me.

Packers at Oxford and Crisfield paid shuckers as high as $3.50 a day for twenty gallons of oysters. As soon as a shucker filled her bucket, she took it to a window that opened into the packing house. There a man called a "skimmer" poured the bucket of oysters into a large strainer and then washed them off with fresh water. He then scooped up the oysters into a quart measure and poured them into a large tub of cold water. A record was kept of every gallon of oysters handed through the window, and workers received a brass check for each gallon shucked. At the end of the day packers paid twenty cents for every brass check held by the shucker.

Throughout the 1870s the oyster packers of the Eastern Shore shipped nine million bushels annually. In the 1877-1878 season Crisfield alone shipped twenty-five thousand barrels of shell oysters and three hundred thousand gallons of shucked oysters to Baltimore and New York. Packing houses like those operated by Isaac Coulbourn, John Lee Carmon, and J. H. Goodsell were hives of activity. Packers paid watermen twenty-five cents a bushel; a bushel usually produced a gallon of oysters. The same gallon that cost them forty-five cents to buy and shuck, packers sold for a dollar. With such high profits at stake, packers sought to outbid and outmaneuver their competitors. Isaac Tawes, like most shrewd packers, kept his invoice book of urban wholesalers under lock and key to prevent being underbid by a rival. When oysters were in short supply, packers diluted their kegs of oysters with large amounts of water and ice and told their customers that oysters could only be savored with large amounts of "likker." Although the industry attracted many would-be entrepreneurs, oystering was a rough business. Competition was stiff, and packers argued, haggled, and connived for good oysters, good shuckers, and good customers. They also had to contend with railroad and steamship agents who rarely had adequate labor to load oysters for shipment. Many packing houses folded or changed hands annually, and cautious local businessmen invested in real estate, hardware stores, and saloons rather than hazard the rough-and-tumble of the oyster trade. "On the Eastern Shore," complained Christopher Nelson, captain of the oyster schooner *Florence*, "it was the shop keepers and dry goods merchants that made the money" from the oyster boom.

During the season of 1869-1870 there were 563 vessels licensed in Maryland to dredge for oysters; they averaged twenty-three tons each and carried eight hundred bushels at a load. Despite the law prohibiting out-of-state dredgers, many outsiders registered their vessels under Maryland owners with false bills of sale. These dredges employed 2,107 white men and 1,453 blacks. Another 3,325 whites and blacks were employed on smaller boats; and about 10,000 were involved in the land operations side of the industry. The economic impact of the boom was especially noticeable along Baltimore's Long Wharf, where hundreds of schooners, pungies, and bateaux annually disgorged four million bushels of oysters to the insatiable packing houses. Every neighborhood in Baltimore had its oyster bays in cool rooms where oyster sellers always had fresh "selects" from the Eastern Shore. On Federal Hill at the Washington Monument, old black men sold oysters from two-gallon buckets— one in each hand; their street cry of "Ohie! Ohie! Oysters fine and cheap!" always attracted customers.

The American and foreign demand for oysters advanced faster than the supply. The avalanche of orders from the mining camps of Colorado and the restaurants of San Francisco overwhelmed Maryland packers. To assure their supply, several San Francisco merchants purchased four thousand bushels of oysters and had them shipped around Cape Horn from St. Michaels to be planted in the waters of California. As James Richardson concluded in *Scribner's Magazine* in 1877, "If every acre of available coast water, from Cape Cod to the mouth of the Chesapeake were brought under cultivation, it is doubtful whether the supply of oysters could even outrun the demand." Added another Maryland observer, "Nobody tires of oysters. Raw, roasted, scalded, stewed, fried, broiled, escalloped, in pâtes, in fritters, in soup, oysters are found on every table, sometimes at every meal, and yet no entertainment is complete without them."

The Eastern Shore waterman at his tiller on the Bay tended to experience the vagaries of the oyster industry in the same manner that he endured the weather; there were good packers and bad ones, and occasionally it seemed that they, like the icy weather of a winter season, were leagued against him. Yet most watermen were good-natured and accepted a life of continuous struggle as long as they were permitted to sell oysters on a strictly cash basis and no one attempted to take away their freedom. In the late nineteenth century the Eastern Shore's five thousand watermen were divided into two principal groups, dredgers and tongers. The first group,

Baltimore oyster peddler, *Harper's Weekly*, March 2, 1889.

called "drudgers" by local folks, used large sailing vessels to pull the basketlike scoop across the beds. Although dredging had originally been prohibited on the Bay, Maryland counties gradually liberalized their laws, and after the Civil War dredgers could operate on the Chesapeake as long as they remained in deep water. By the 1870s, however, the dredging fleet acquired notoriety for defying local oyster laws and poaching oysters in shallow county waters.

The typical Eastern Shore waterman, though, tonged for oysters, using a small sailboat that needed only one or two men. The most characteristic tonging boat in the late nineteenth century was a round-bottomed craft formed from three dug-out logs joined together. This craft had one or two sails and generally a jib and no deck. These boats were from eight to twenty-five feet long and were quite seaworthy.

Men working on a tong boat divided the labor between them, one tonging while the other culled the oysters that were too small. The waterman seized the handles of his tongs and allowed the heavy irons to slip down into the water until the handles stood up vertically before him. By spreading the handles apart, he opened the teeth. After opening and closing them several times until he felt that he had a good batch of oysters, he slowly raised the tongs and dumped the catch on the culling board. As soon as the board was full, the culler picked up his hammer and began to break the clusters of oysters. After a time the culler and the tonger changed places. In the shallows of Tangier Sound and at the mouths of the Chester and Choptank rivers, the little boats anchored over the beds and bobbed lazily as their crews busily engaged with the tongs and called to one another from boat to boat.

Watermen could distinguish one boat from another at a glance and tell the boat's port county by the cut of the sail, the rake of the mast, and as one native put it, "by patterns more felt than seen." About three o'clock in the afternoon the log canoes would head for a buy boat displaying a bushel basket on its mast. The basket signaled that the captain was buying oysters, and the buy boat was soon surrounded by

Eating oysters on the dock, *Harper's Weekly*, March 2, 1889.

sailing craft, like a hen with a flock of young chicks. The buy boat saved watermen the trouble of freighting their own oysters and made a profit of ten to fifteen cents a bushel in carrying the oysters to Baltimore.

The tongers went out early in the morning, and it was almost dark before they returned. Many waterfront towns like St. Michaels were almost abandoned by their male populations during the day. The night, however, was likely to be lively—especially if the steamer *Olive* carried the dollar jugs of Baltimore whiskey that watermen used to fortify themselves against the cold. St. Michaels always buzzed with excitement when the steamer came into view. In the words of a local inhabitant, "A queen and her imperial train could not have received more homage than the sidewheeler from Baltimore." Children raced to the wharf at the sound of the steamer's whistle, and the boat soon came splashing to rest at the wharf. Roustabouts rushed here and there loading and unloading cargo while passengers disembarked. Shortly thereafter, a shrill whistle sounded, the waters churned, and in a few minutes the steamer had rounded the bend in the river. While jug whiskey was one of their few contacts with American urban life, many watermen dreamed of going "whole hog" on a steamboat holiday to Baltimore.

Although oyster boats under sail on the Bay were picturesque, the actual business of tonging was physically exhausting. As oystering was a winter occupation, watermen were chilled by the freezing water splashed up by the tongs. Handling cold and wet oysters on the culling board caused severe cramps and fatigue. Only the hardiest could stand such a rigorous life, and the death rate among oystermen was very high. Rheumatism and other infirmities caused by a life of extreme physical labor and constant exposure to the elements took their toll. Such risks made watermen fatalistic, and most aimed no higher in life than to get through the winter months. Reckless of the future, they lived for the moment. In the summer months many oystermen turned to fishing or farming. Complex in habit and attitude, watermen were also clannish, secretive about their business, and suspicious of outsiders. Paradoxically, in local community life they were viewed as both freedom-loving mariners and shiftless rogues.

In the 1870s St. Michaels was a disorderly village known more for its hard-living watermen than for its important role in the Chesapeake during the War of 1812. Among the Negro shanties that flanked the harbor's edge a waterman of either race could pursue fancies that ranged from a woman to conjuration and witchcraft. Although gentry like the Lloyds and smooth-talking Easton lawyers still dominated the politics of Talbot County, they could not control the headstrong oystermen of St. Michaels. No prosecuting attorney could convict a St. Michaels oysterman of murder, townsmen remarked, because all of his relatives would be on the jury.

Harbor life was confined to an intricate web of planks and walkways that went past piles of oyster shells to the sand and mud alley that led to the business section of the village. Most oystermen lived in three-room houses that were an easy stroll from their boats. During cold weather men and women dressed by the kitchen stove, and the nightly ordeal of going to bed in winter was preceded by an elaborate ceremony of putting on numerous layers of clothing. Like their men, the women of this maritime community were often crude and blunt in social response. Those women who didn't smoke a pipe rubbed snuff. As with most communities of the Chesapeake, local watermen were greatly preoccupied with nicknames, and the elegant appellations of the Old Testament retreated before the familiar names of Owl, Mousey, Buster, Hopalong, and Lightning. Watermen didn't believe in education, and thought it a tool of the devil. Many St. Michaels oystermen were case-hardened cynics who believed in a harsh life and a stern God who served as a vengeful overlord of the Chesapeake's inland sea.

St. Michaels' black watermen were known throughout the Eastern Shore. Following emancipation, these broad-shouldered, aquiline-featured oystermen worked as steve-

Dredgers at the hand windlass. Courtesy: The Baltimore *Sun*.

dores, crew members on steamboats, and ship pilots. Like most blacks on the Bay at this time, they harvested oysters in winter, netted shad in the spring, and freighted watermelons and tomatoes in their sloops to Baltimore during summer. Generally they were known as good sailors and enterprising businessmen. Like the whites, black watermen had their own violent code of behavior, and packers who cheated them were occasionally murdered. The uncertainties of a waterman's life prompted black women to fear the Chesapeake as an evil and mysterious place. "Don't you start him drudgin' and tongin' oysters," prayed many a black mother as she nursed her infant son.

Unlike the tongers, the men who manned the dredge boats considered the entire Chesapeake their province. Piloting schooners of ten tons or more with a deep keel and a flush deck, the captains of the dredge boats earned much more money with their oyster scoops than the tongers. Dredging, like tonging, was an unpleasant and difficult occupation. The crew lived in a cramped, smoky cabin on board and subsisted on coarse fare. When the dredge boats reached the oyster beds in deep water, the crew let the dredge drop overboard and at the same time let the rope run out behind. In this manner the dredge, or scoop, was dragged across the oyster bar. The iron teeth of the dredge dug into the oyster bed, and the scoop was soon full. Then the crew turned to the difficult task of winding up the rope on a hand-turned windlass. Samuel T. Sewell, who worked on Chesapeake dredge boats at the turn of the century, remembered the ordeal of the hand windlass. "In my time," he recalled, "we used handwinders to bring the oysters on deck. And it was backbreaking work from sunrise to sundown." There were usually two windlasses, one on the port and one on the starboard amidships. Each windlass required the labor of four men. As the dredge filled with oysters, the crew would wind the cable around the drum of the windlass and bring the dredge on deck. The dredge was so heavy that Sewell described it as "like pulling in anchor while the boat was sailing." Understandably, the dredge boat captains had difficulty keeping their crews. Millard Tawes of Crisfield remembered that his father signed on to dredge oysters in the 1880s. "My father lasted exactly one day on that dredge boat before he quit," Tawes said. "It was inhuman work and my father was not about to ruin himself for oysters." Profits from dredging oysters were divided by thirds. The boat was awarded a third for maintenance and repairs, the captain received a third, and the crew got a third. The boats usually left Crisfield and other ports on Monday morning and returned early Friday afternoon with their catch.

At first relations between tongers and dredgers had been fairly amicable. By 1871, however, nearly a thousand dredge boats began to invade the prohibited river waters of the Chesapeake. While the outraged tongers demanded that Annapolis enforce the law preventing dredging in the rivers, they also took the law into their own hands. When they went out on the water, tongers warned, they would have their rifles loaded. Soon the Chesapeake resounded to gunfire, and a Baltimore *Sun* reporter noted that something new was floating in the Chester and Choptank rivers—the bloated bodies of dead oystermen.

Chapter 2

HUNTER DAVIDSON
& THE OYSTER POLICE

C APTAIN HUNTER DAVIDSON, commander of the Maryland Oyster Navy, stood in the pilot house of his armored side-wheel steamer *Leila* as the vessel docked at Oxford. The winter oyster season of 1869-1870 had been uncommonly severe, and even though it was late March the cold wind cut easily through Davidson's naval coat. A sudden storm howling across the Chesapeake had forced Davidson and his men into port after several frustrating days of trying to police a twelve-mile square of hell known as Eastern Bay. Lying between Queen Anne's and Talbot counties, Eastern Bay had erupted into violence as tongers and dredgers resorted to their Winchester rifles to decide who would pull oysters out of its shallow waters. The *Leila* was a worn-out Civil War tug that had been used to chase blockade runners on the Chesapeake. Its boiler was so decrepit that the ship could only proceed at half steam and caused Davidson as much trouble as the marauders on the Bay.

Few turned out at Oxford to welcome either Captain Davidson or the *Leila*. The Oyster Navy, chartered by the Maryland General Assembly to police the industry and bring law and order to the Bay in 1868, was very unpopular with Eastern Shoremen. They viewed the Oyster Navy as a frivolous waste of tax money that prevented people from earning a living; and while the assembly didn't bow to their demands for the Navy's abolition, neither did it provide funds for the efficient operation of the flotilla.

THE OYSTER WARS

After two years as commander of the Oyster Navy, Davidson was accustomed to the hostile glare of oystermen. In earlier times the tall and genial Kent Islander had been welcome at Oxford, but on this raw March day only two black watermen awaited him at the end of the dock. While tonging for oysters in the Choptank River, they had pulled up the bodies of three Negroes who had been chained together and had their skulls crushed. Unless Davidson and his men did something to quell violence on the rivers, they urged, small-scale oystermen wouldn't have a chance. With oysters commanding forty-five cents a bushel, many boats crowded the bars of the Wye, Choptank, and Miles rivers; and hardly a week went by without a violent death on the water. A spirit of anarchy prevailed on the Chesapeake, and Davidson had only fifty men to police a Bay of several hundred square miles and countless coves and inlets. There were several hundred swift-sailing dredges on the Bay, and during the season Davidson had made only forty arrests.

At the 1869 legislative budget hearings Davidson had pleaded for more money and better vessels. "It is impossible with my current force," he told the state oyster commission, "to police an area that ranges from Swan Point, Kent County, down to the Potomac and up river 125 miles." The oyster vessels were manned by uneducated and daring men who were "reckless of consequences;" and the industry was "more like a scramble for something adrift, where the object of everyone appears [to be] to get as much as he can before it is lost." The demand for oysters as an article of export, Davidson added, "has so stimulated the trade in the Chesapeake that oystermen will risk any weather and are willing to kill to enable them to reach the handsome profits that are now being offered them in the market."

The mathematics of the oyster industry revealed in telling detail why the dredge boats were invading the rivers and why watermen were getting killed. Davidson carried the figures with him wherever he went:

38

Cost of a dredging vessel	$800
Wear and tear of boat	100
Crew	700
Food and fuel	300
Total for 1869	$1,900

During the course of the 1869-1870 season Davidson esti-
mated that a dredging vessel would catch 11,200 bushels of
oysters, which at a conservative thirty-five cents a bushel
amounted to $3,920. With a captain's profit of $2,000 in a
year when most Marylanders earned $500 or less, oystering
was one of the most profitable trades in the state. The legislature, though, remained unmoved by Hunter Davidson's testimony. The Democrat-controlled legislature, led by Baltimore boss Isaac Raisin, was happily distributing patronage
jobs and looting the state treasury. The Oyster Navy lacked
popularity as well as a constituency of voters that could be
bought, and friends advised Hunter Davidson not to risk his
life on Chesapeake Bay for the "corruptionists of Annapolis."

The Byzantine maneuverings in Annapolis worked in
strange ways, however. As the fall of 1870 approached, the
Baltimore American published several articles deploring the
"outlawry" on Chesapeake Bay. The Raisin machine sensed
that a law-and-order issue would be good for Democrats in
the election in the following spring and siphoned funds from
the state Department of Agriculture to expand and improve
Davidson's flotilla and equip each boat with a Hotchkiss
Rapid Firing Gun. Toward the end of September twelve sailing vessels and one steamer proudly displayed the flag of the
Maryland Oyster Navy in Annapolis harbor. Davidson hired
new crews for the patrols and was especially pleased by the
recruitment of Captain James Clements to the force. A so-
cially well-connected Bay pilot with family in Baltimore and
on the Eastern Shore, Clements helped his commander purchase the *Mary Compton*, a sturdy Bay schooner. Working
together, Davidson and Clements pestered the state militia
for surplus weapons and scored a triumph with the acquisi-

Black watermen, *Harper's Weekly*, March 10, 1872.

tion of a howitzer, which they promptly installed in the bow of the *Mary Compton*.

Captain Robert H. McCready was another welcome addition to the Oyster Navy. An adventurous mariner from Somerset County, McCready commanded the police sloop *Avalon*, and at the beginning of the 1871 oyster season captured six boats that were illegally dredging in the Wicomico River. The outlaw dredgers were taken to Deal's Island and fined fifty dollars each by Justice of the Peace George T. Rowe. Stiff fines and a visible police presence on the Bay, McCready claimed, were the first steps toward restoring order to the oyster industry. Good weapons and an ample supply of ammunition also helped. Later that winter several oystermen disappeared near Crisfield, and their dead bodies were found floating in the Annemessex River. From Annapolis Davidson telegraphed McCready that he was sending the *Mary Compton* into Tangier Sound with instructions to fire upon any dredge boat resisting seizure by the oyster police.

In April 1872, the *Mary Compton* spied several dredgers illegally pulling up oysters in the mouth of the Annemessex River. Through a hand megaphone Captain Clements yelled, "Heave to and stand by for boarding!" The pirates replied with their rifles, and Clements flung himself to the deck as gunfire riddled the vessel. Regaining control of his schooner, Clements ordered the howitzer loaded, and on the next turn the *Compton* blasted a dredge at close quarters. The boat quickly sank and the pirates escaped to shore. Another shot from the *Compton* widely missed the escaping dredgers. The wind had begun to toss the Bay, and it was impossible to fire accurately from the pitching boat. Although the oyster police captured no one, reported the Salisbury *Advertiser*, they did at least show a new authority on the Chesapeake.

Shortly thereafter, Captain Davidson sent the *Mary Compton* to the mouth of the Chester River, and Captain Clements became an anathema to dredgers as he filled the Chestertown jail with river rogues. Clements also gained a reputation as a killer. As the *Mary Compton* could easily be outdistanced by many of the faster sailing oyster boats, Clements often shot fleeing oystermen with his rifle. In the process he killed two oystermen from Long Island Sound, and the *New York Times* complained that "the oyster police seem to regard the dredgers as pirates to be shot down and murdered on the sightest provocation." Clements, though, was acting in strict accordance to the instructions of his commander. Hunter Davidson was determined to quell the outlaw dredgers and use the Oyster Navy to impose order on this volatile industry. With his sidewheeler *Leila* now restored to good running condition, Davidson was so ubiquitous on the Bay that he kept the oyster pirates in a constant state of anxiety.

Throughout January 1871, the *Leila* routinely cruised the Chesapeake between Annapolis and Cambridge. Though ice was beginning to cluster in large floating pieces, the Bay was still accessible to maritime commerce. The slate-gray sky added a stark perspective to the Bay, and both the Chesapeake and the shoreline looked as if they had been etched in charcoal by an artist. In the galley of the *Leila*, the ship's cook busily prepared hot meals of fried ham, beans, and biscuits for the crew and bubbled as happily as his coffee pot over word that he would soon be seeing his family in St. Michaels.

When the Bay began to ice up and the cruel northwest wind made oystering intolerable on open water, many watermen headed toward St. Michaels and the gentle waters of the Miles River. Watermen could easily break through the thin ice and tong for oysters with their sixteen-foot shafts. They traded for salt beef and potatoes with local farmers and found shelter in the river's coves. It was here in the safe anchorage of the Miles that several pirate crews of oyster dredge boats, plotted Captain Davidson's murder. The scheme was simple. Late at night while the *Leila* rested at anchor, the pirates would steal upon the boat in a small skiff, quietly board it, and kill him.

HUNTER DAVIDSON & THE OYSTER POLICE

Shortly after midnight on January 28, 1871, a small boat left St. Michaels, staying close to the shore to avoid being silhouetted on the open water. As the pirates eased their way through the ice cakes and approached the steamer they discovered only one man on duty; they quickly knocked him unconscious with a culling hammer. When they arrived at Davidson's cabin they discovered that the door was locked, and as they struggled with it, they awakened the captain. With hardly a moment to lose, Davidson leaped out of bed, grabbed his Colt revolver, and fired two shots through the door. The pirates scrambled desperately back to their skiff and were rowing wildly for the shore when Davidson fixed them in the sight of his rifle. After a short burst of fire over their heads, the oystermen surrendered and Davidson's men brought the criminals back to the *Leila* in shackles. While Davidson had foiled Gus Rice's plan and had arrested several of his men, this would not be the last time that the oyster police would have to fight the wily oyster pirate. Later that day in St. Michaels, Davidson wearily confessed to a state fisheries inspector that when he first went to sea he never dreamed that anyone would try to kill him over an oyster.

By 1872 the disputes among watermen had intensified to a point where the Oyster Navy permanently placed armed schooners at the mouth of the Manokin River, Hoopers Straits, Honga River, and Swan Point off Rock Hall. Each police boat had a crew of three, and the captain received a salary of fifty dollars a month while the crewmen drew thirty dollars. Each man also received thirty cents a day from the legislature for rations and fifty rounds of ammunition per month. Somerset County, in addition, maintained its own armed vessel in the mouth of the Wicomico River. Under Davidson's forceful supervision, the Oyster Navy arrested over 130 men and fined them $7,352 for illegal dredging. These fines were used to finance the Oyster Navy and relieved Hunter Davidson of the onerous task of soliciting funds from the state legislature.

Above, Police pursue oyster pirates, *Harper's Weekly*, March 1, 1884. *Below*,
Pirates dredging at night, *Harper's Weekly*, March 1, 1884.

Many ship captains complained that the Oyster Navy gave all the dredge boats a bad name. Most of the dredgers, they argued, obeyed state and county laws and cooperated with Maryland fisheries officials. In their view Hunter Davidson was overzealous in his enforcement of the law and put the needs of the Oyster Navy ahead of the industry it was supposed to serve. While there were admittedly pirates on the oyster bars, there were also proud and widely respected men like Jacob Wesley Webster of Deal's Island on the dredges.

A staunch Methodist and keen-eyed sailor, Jake Webster in 1871 was captain of the *Bessie Woolford*, a ten-ton oyster sloop, and leader of the seventy-vessel dredging fleet at Deal's Island. The *Woolford* was a trim boat, well fitted for oyster dredging, but for pleasure sailing her quarters were rather constrained. When seated at "grub" in the cabin below deck, Webster could reach the coffee pot from the stove without leaving the table. There were berths on each side of the cabin and in the stern; they were, Woolford joked, about "as high as an unabridged dictionary," but were two men deep. The *Woolford* had a crew of four, one of whom served as the cook.

As the *Woolford* made her start along the creek lined with high salt grass and cattails, the mast and sails of the vessel seemed to be coming up from the land. The sloop moved out into Tangier Sound, not without company. The Sound was alive with a fleet of nearly two hundred vessels whose unfurled sails made the dredge boats resemble a powerful armada. The September weather was brilliant as the sunlight danced upon the crystal waves and dispelled the mists that hung over the tangled marshes. The wind came up, and Captain Webster yanked the tiller, awakening the boat and sending her plunging impetuously across the Sound toward the Great Rocks oyster bar. The *Woolford* took her place among the dredges, and the crew now began the earnest business of "licking the bar." In Chesapeake Bay metaphor the dredges were the "tongues" of the boat, which "licked" plenty of oysters. The practiced eye of a veteran oysterman like Jake Webster could tell at a glance a poor lick from a good one. Each boat displayed a black-and-white license number so that the oyster police would know that it wasn't a renegade vessel. One of the crew removed the wooden cranks from the winder before he flung the dredge into the water and let the chain go. Otherwise the cranks might fly off after a revolution or two and kill someone.

As Webster brought the ship to, the crew began cranking the winder furiously; when the rattling chain ceased, the hands gathered at the side of the vessel to see the result of the catch. "Dump the dredge, Joe!" Webster yelled, and the great iron maw was hauled aboard over the roller and its gathering spread upon the deck. Fish and crabs squirmed helplessly as the cook grabbed a seafood supper from the scoop. The oysters were then culled and the refuse shoveled back into the Bay. After several licks at the bar, Webster noted that the oysters were "trashy looking" and not like the fat oysters of previous seasons. Later that night Webster's suspicions that the "rocks" were being looted at night by Virginia watermen were confirmed by the other captains. While Maryland dredgers and tongers quarreled, the Virginians stole upon the bars of Tangier Sound and sailed off with the treasure. There were times, Webster reflected bitterly, when those who obeyed the oyster laws and worked hard were just damned fools.

Virginia did not enforce the federal law requiring its watermen to remain in their own territorial waters, and many Virginia oystermen poached oysters in the Maryland beds. Also, the lack of a definitive agreement between Maryland and Virginia regarding a boundary line across the Bay to the Potomac River was a constant source of friction. Before the Civil War and the emergence of the oyster industry, a modern trans-Chesapeake boundary line was considered unnecessary. After 1870, however, the boundary question became a burning issue.

The controversy between the two states dated back to 1668, when an agreement was entered into by Philip Calvert on the part of Maryland and Colonel Edmund Scarborough of Virginia. Under this compact Virginia received fifteen thousand more acres of territory than Maryland eventually thought she was entitled to. In 1785 the compact was renegotiated and representatives from the two states met with General George Washington at his plantation at Mount Vernon to iron out their difficulties. The primary issue at this time centered on equal access for both states to the waters of the Potomac River. The new agreement acknowledged Maryland's sovereignty over the Potomac but gave Virginia equal access to the river. The new agreement allowed for reciprocal rights in the Pocomoke River on the Eastern Shore as well. The Compact of 1785 prevailed until the Civil War. By 1870, however, the Pocomoke Sound was one of the richest areas in the Bay in oysters and the focus of complicated litigation. Did Maryland watermen, on the basis of their right to fish in the Pocomoke River, have the right to harvest oysters in the Virginia sections of the Pocomoke Sound? Maryland oystermen insisted that the entire Pocomoke Sound was a natural extension of the Pocomoke River and that Maryland was therefore allowed access to the oyster beds. Virginia vigorously disagreed and argued that Maryland did not have access to the Pocomoke Sound. The 1785 pact referred only to the Pocomoke River and therefore, said Virginia, Maryland was entitled to harvest oysters only in that part of the Sound under its jurisdiction. With lives and fortunes at stake, this was hardly an academic question.

A second, related issue affected the economic well-being of the port of Crisfield, as well as the livelihoods of hundreds of Somerset County watermen. Where was the real boundary line across the Chesapeake Bay? According to Maryland's calculations, the boundary line went from low watermark of the southern shore of the Potomac from Smith's Point to the mouth of the Pocomoke River. Virginia hotly dissented. To have agreed to Maryland's interpretation of the boundary would have meant Virginia's surrender of about forty square miles of oyster grounds in Tangier Sound. On June 1, 1872, commissioners from the two states met at Crisfield to begin negotiating a satisfactory settlement of the boundary question. The Virginia commissioners, led by General Henry A. Wise, demanded a boundary line that, if established, would have given Virginia a large slice of the little Annemessex River, half of Crisfield, twenty miles of Tangier Sound, and a large part of Smith Island. Maryland responded with an equally outrageous demand. Throughout that summer, each state blustered and the boundary negotiations became stalemated. Finally, in 1874, the oyster industry's demand for a well-demarcated boundary line prompted the two states to refer their dispute to federal arbitration.

After three years of complicated negotiations, a boundary line was finally determined. Under the Jenkins-Black Award of 1877 the boundary was demarcated as beginning at a point on the Potomac where the line between Virginia and West Virginia strikes the river at low watermark; thence to Smith's Point and across the Bay to Watkins Point on the Pocomoke. In terms of oyster beds, Virginia got the larger share of the Tangier and Pocomoke sounds, and Marylanders who ran over the "line of '77" to take oysters ran the risk of being captured by Virginia police and having their boats confiscated. Although Maryland retained sovereignty over the famous Great Rocks, the Award of 1877 embittered large numbers of Maryland watermen. They had lost access to many of the oyster beds in the Pocomoke Sound upon which their prosperity had rested.

Somerset watermen also complained that Virginia still did nothing to prevent its dredge boats from crossing the line and stealing oysters in Maryland waters. Virginia boats, Isaac Lawson of Somerset complained, were depleting many of the beds reserved for local tongers. Just when the tongers had begun to have difficulties keeping Maryland dredge boats out of their oyster beds, the Virginians had also begun to steal their oysters. Finally Lawson, L. T. Dryden, and other citizens of Somerset County went to Annapolis on December 6, 1883, and demanded the intervention of the Oyster Navy.

Inasmuch as the state refused to assist them out of reluctance to rekindle the old boundary dispute, Somerset's watermen decided to take the law into their own hands. Throughout December, 1883, invading Virginia dredges encountered a storm of bullets from outraged Maryland watermen, and for the remainder of the season open warfare prevailed. To retaliate against the Virginia poachers, the watermen of Smith Island pirated oysters in Virginia waters. When the Virginia police schooner *Tangier* pursued the watermen back to Smith Island, it met a fierce reception. The schooner was fired upon from shore by twenty-five Marylanders with repeating rifles. The *Tangier* returned the fire with a salvo from its cannon. The Smith Islanders fired five hundred rounds or more and threw up hasty breastworks to protect the island from invasion by the Virginia police. Promising a fight to the finish, the Marylanders defied Captain A. J. Read to come ashore. Outnumbered and reluctant to storm the fortifications on the island, Read and his men sailed the *Tangier* back to port at Onancock, Virginia.

To a great extent the conflict between Virginians and Marylanders grew out of a steadily decreasing supply of available oysters that resulted from the overfishing of the oyster bars by dredge boats. As early as 1870 Hunter Davidson in his *Report upon the Oyster Resources of Maryland* had warned that the oyster resources of the lower Bay were being recklessly depleted as oystermen disregarded the culling laws. The popular attitude on Chesapeake Bay, Davidson summarized, was reflected in the folk saying, "Get it today! Hell with tamar! Leave it till tamar, somebody else'll get it." The lack of adequate oyster reserves, Davidson added, forced Somerset dredgers to raid the waters of other counties.

Championing the oystermen was a good way to win votes, and politicians and judges were lenient toward watermen who violated the oyster laws. One oyster policeman who arrested a dredger for stealing from a river bar reported that the conversation between the judge and the waterman went like this:

"Son," said the judge, "wasn't you in my Sunday school class when you was a boy?"

"Yessir. I was in your class all right," the waterman responded.

"That's what I thought. A boy like you couldn't possibly be guilty of anything serious. Case dismissed."

In Kent County, local politicians went up and down the Chester River in their sail boats giving watermen cigars and liquor "to oil a few votes." In turn, the polling places at the Chestertown firehall were crowded with half-drunk oystermen. The oyster interests were staunchly defended in Annapolis by Kent's legislators, and an oysterman who got out the vote received a contract to pave a street with oyster shells, or a bridge tender's job.

Before long the Oyster Navy felt the powerful grip of the Democratic octopus in Annapolis. Isaac Raisin ordered his chieftains to find sinecures for loyal Democrats, and the Oyster Navy was ripe for patronage appointments. Hunter Davidson was helpless before the might of the Democratic party and resigned his commission as commander of the Oyster Navy in disgust. Following Davidson's resignation, the Oyster Navy became an extension of the Democratic machine. William Timmons, the new commander, did not share his predecessor's conservationist attitudes and de-emphasized the Oyster Navy's role in policing the Bay. The state legislature lost interest in maintaining a strong oyster flotilla, and by 1884 *Harper's* reported that of the hundred men in the Oyster Navy, "not more than a dozen were efficient." Most of the oyster police were interested only in the pay, and one captain resigned his commission when it appeared that he would have to confront the dredgers. Telegraphing the naval militia at Annapolis, the man said, "During the Civil War I paid $300 for a substitute and at my time of life I have too much self-respect to allow myself to be shot by an oyster pirate." Other captains in the Oyster Navy simply heaved to and went home when fired upon by the oyster pirates. Besides, the oyster dredgers were better sailors than the police. When the night was dark, the wind blowing hard, and icy slush formed on the deck, few captains in the Maryland Oyster Navy had the inclination to hazard their lives against the pirates on the billowing Chesapeake.

Throughout the 1870s the legislature's interest in the resources of the Chesapeake Bay rose and fell with the election returns. In 1876, a stormy presidential election year for Maryland and the nation, the General Assembly of Maryland became worried about the future supply of oysters in the Bay and commissioned a survey of Tangier Sound, the most productive oyster region in the Chesapeake. In the late nineteenth century oceanographic research was still in its infancy, and there were very few men who could make the kind of study that the legislature required. After several weeks of negotiations, however, Maryland finally prevailed upon the United States Navy to allow the state to have the services of one of its marine surveyors for six months.

On October 15, 1878, Lieutenant Francis Winslow, USN, reported for duty at the naval militia headquarters in Annapolis. After only four years in the navy, the handsome and taciturn New Englander had established a reputation as one of the best marine surveyors and chart makers in the service. A light autumn rain cast the town in a gray mist as Lieutenant Winslow walked down the hill from the State House to the seedy waterfront of tin-roofed warehouses. The little harbor was full of skiffs and oyster sloops, a sign in the early afternoon that the waters of the Bay were being churned by the remnants of a storm that had blown up the coast from Hatteras. Standing on the police dock, Winslow studied the boat that would soon be his home, a large steam-powered sidewheeler that had the features of a steamboat of the lower Mississippi. On board, the ship appeared to be in good condition: the cabins were bright and spacious, the galley well equipped, and the crew members informed about Winslow's mission.

"She's called the *Leila*, sir," volunteered one of the crew. "And she'll suit your purpose nicely."

51

THE OYSTER WARS

Before embarking on his survey, however, Winslow was told by Captain James Langrall of the oyster police to exercise great caution on Tangier Sound. "Life is cheap down there," he warned. "Them Somerset drudgers don't like outsiders on the bars." Langrall had experienced his share of violent encounters with the dredgers of Somerset. As captain of the schooner *Regulator* in 1873, Langrall had been hired by Dorchester County to patrol the mouth of the Choptank River to discourage oyster pirates from Somerset County. During one skirmish, Langrall and his deputies killed two Deal's Island watermen. In the weeks that ensued feelings between the counties were so intense that the *Baltimore American* reported a civil war on the lower Chesapeake.

Until Winslow's appointment, only one man, Paul DeBroca, had conducted a wide-ranging investigation of the oysters of Chesapeake Bay. The French government had sent the famous zoologist to Maryland in 1860 in order to discover ways of rejuvenating France's declining oyster industry; like DeBroca, Lieutenant Winslow would amass a considerable amount of scientific data on the Bay. On October 20, 1878, the *Leila* slipped out of Annapolis and headed southward. Winslow turned the *Leila* into a floating biological and cartographic laboratory; old Bay charts, boxes of sample tubes, drafting instruments, steamboat time tables, and culling hammers cluttered the ship's salon. On deck lay eighteen fathoms of chain used to take soundings and collect samples from the bottom of the Bay, several pairs of oyster tongs, and a small dredge.

The Chesapeake contrasted sharply with Winslow's rock-swept New England coast. The Eastern Shore of Maryland offered a panorama of prosperous farms and manicured plantations that hugged the water's edge; thick forests of walnut, oak, and pine made the wilderness seem like the retreat of ancient Druids. At the wide river mouths of the Bay Winslow discovered vast expanses of salt marsh, the homes of herons, kingfishers, and marsh wrens. Across the marshes turkey buzzards circled above the pines lazily riding the winds on motionless wings. As Winslow noted, the direction of the wind largely determined the weather of Chesapeake Bay. North and northeast winds brought clear, cold weather; winds from the south brought warm weather, even in midwinter. Given the variability of the winds, temperatures in the region could change suddenly from extreme cold to extreme warmth. At times Winslow watched dredge boats come about in fierce winds, and he marveled at how easily the crews managed their rolling craft. Southeast winds brought dangerous squalls and electrical storms that hastened watermen to safe anchorage.

Winslow had cordial relations with his men, and in the days that followed the crew worked energetically to unlock the secrets of Tangier Sound. Winslow was particularly interested in examining the baby oysters that were brought up on deck. They were, he claimed, a fairly good prediction of future harvests. While the *Leila* methodically sampled the bars, few dredge boats were hindered in their work, and the suspicions of the watermen yielded to an amused curiosity as day after day they saw Winslow and his men at work with their sounding chain and oyster dredge.

Far from being the *enfants terribles* that he had been warned to expect, Winslow found the watermen good-natured and helpful. Often in reference to a particular bar a waterman would call out to Winslow, "What does she look like, Captain?" Winslow had only bad news for the watermen. In his extremely detailed and mathematically precise analysis of Tangier Sound, Winslow found only one oyster to three square yards of beds. Such low yields confirmed Winslow's theory that the beds were being exhausted. In later reports Winslow called attention to the fact that the oyster was not an endless resource. The lax enforcement of culling laws that prevented removal of young oysters less than three inches in length as well as the failure to reseed the beds with oyster shells, he warned, would doom the industry unless reforms were made. Oysters were being taken out of the Bay at a rate far greater than they could be replenished by natural reproduction.

Most watermen, however, disregarded these gloomy findings. The 1880s would be a decade of record oyster catches on the Bay, and few dredgers cared that their own rapacity would ruin the industry. Simply put, there was too much money to be made catching oysters to think of conservation. The dredgers lived by the wind, and neither the oyster police nor marine-life surveys would deter these "water arabs" from looting the Bay.

Chapter 3

PADDIES & WATER ARABS

URING THE 1880s the oyster boom on the Chesapeake
was at its height. In 1884, the peak year for the industry, watermen harvested a record fifteen million
bushels of oysters. A reporter for *Harper's* described the
boom as "simply a mad scramble carried on in 700 boats
manned by 5,600 daring and unscrupulous men." The dredging crews of the Chesapeake at this time, added Dr. Walter
Wyman of Baltimore's Maritime Hospital, were "motley in
character, some of them colored, a few criminals, and many
of them foreigners but recently arrived, scarcely able to speak
the English language." This latter immigrant group formed
the bulk of the water-borne oyster work force. Ignorant of
American ways, these "Paddies," as they were called after
the Irish, were beguiled into signing on a dredge boat with the
promise of ample food, satisfactory working conditions, and
good pay. Once on board the men were treated unmercifully.
Men were also shanghaied into service. Many German immigrants who had come to New York or Baltimore were
kidnapped and intimidated by brass knuckle and pistol into
manning the windlass on an oyster boat. Until the federal
government intervened to punish sea captains for kidnapping and forced servitude in the oyster industry in 1907,
slavery flourished on Chesapeake Bay. The story of the Paddies constitutes one of the most shameful episodes in Maryland maritime history.

Reports of terrible suffering, cruel treatment, and horrible
murders of Chesapeake dredge-boat crewmen began to reach

Baltimore in the winter of 1881. Most reported these incidents on vessels registered in the counties of Maryland and
Virginia on the lower or southern parts of the Bay. Baltimore
Negroes, after the experience of a few seasons on these oyster
vessels, refused to hire on any more, and newspaper publicity
in the city alerted the home labor market to the evils of the
industry. Thus denied local workers, waterfront shipping
offices applied to large northern cities for men to hire on as
oyster dredgers, promising them reasonable work and fifteen
dollars a month in wages.

During the winter season there were always large numbers of unemployed men who were short of means in New
York and Philadelphia. Shipping agents often recruited immigrants right off the boat at Ellis Island and gave them their
employment card and railroad fare to Baltimore. The shipping agents received two dollars from an oyster dredge captain for every man they induced to sign an agreement, and the
men were not told that their railroad tickets and the two-
dollar commission would be deducted from their wages.
Oyster captains were not particular about their crews. "We
don't care where we get them," bragged Captain Lynn Rea of
the schooner *Ella Agnes*, "whether they are drunk or sober,
clothed or naked, just so they can be made to work at turning
a windlass."

Under the watchful eye of New York shipping agents,
Americans, Irish, Italians, and Germans were taken by rail in
droves from New York to Baltimore. The Paddies usually
arrived at night and were prevented from talking to any
outsiders on the trip. At the Baltimore waterfront they
boarded vessels which took them to the lower Bay for dis-
tribution among the dredge boats. The bewildered men had
to adjust quickly to the harsh realities of life on an oyster
schooner. They began to work at five o'clock in the morning,
received only scarce rations of coarse food, and had to sleep
without bedding in the small forepeak of the boat. Often at
day's end the men were locked below deck to prevent their
escaping, and during the cruise they were not allowed on

A cruel winter for tongers, *Frank Leslie's Illustrated Newspaper*, February 8, 1879.

shore. Most of the captains were armed with pistols and were determined to get as much hard work as possible out of their men. Many Paddies suffered psychological breakdowns and physical collapse from the grueling work and exposure; often the flesh of their hands, after being cut and poisoned by the oyster shells, became violently inflamed. The so-called "oyster hand" was very painful and required months of medical treatment. Each oyster season the Baltimore Marine Hospital treated scores of men who had survived hard service at the mast for frostbite, oyster hand, and broken bones from crank handles on the windlass. Men who refused to work received a cruel beating and were put ashore without pay in a deserted area to make their way back to Baltimore. The lower Eastern Shore of Maryland at this time was a wild and sparsely populated region; and although the state supported the Oyster Navy to protect the oyster beds from unlawful depredation, it had no police to protect the unfortunate Paddies. Stories circulated throughout the region of captains who had shot and killed men on the slightest provocation and afterwards claimed self-preservation in the face of mutiny. Deaths on the Chesapeake were seldom investigated; the federal courts had neither the inclination nor the money to go out on the Bay and arrest offenders. In most cases Baltimore authorities referred the matter to the counties on the Shore, and local judges rarely prosecuted ship captains, no matter how heinous their crimes on the Chesapeake. Murder witnesses often lacked money and a job to enable them to stay in a distant locality for the arrest and trial of the criminal. Being strangers on the Eastern Shore, they were anxious to get to their homes and rejoin their friends.

Occasionally, however, an incident took place which created widespread indignation over the abuse of the Paddies. In December 1884, the horrible murder of a young German immigrant named Otto Mayher marked the beginning of a long struggle by the Maryland German Society and other state civic organizations to protect oyster dredgers from barbarous treatment. This murder was documented in the state courts following the efforts of the German Society to bring Mayher's murderer to trial.

When Otto Mayher signed on the oyster schooner *Eva* for a two-month cruise in October, 1884, he was twenty years old, a hale, hearty-looking fellow with rosy cheeks and a bright healthy appearance. The well-educated son of a Stuttgart surveyor, Mayher had been in Baltimore several weeks looking for work. Mayher was anxious to prove himself in America, and when a German shipping agent offered him a job oystering, he took it. Two weeks later Mayher found himself on board the *Eva* with two other young Germans, Fritz Boye and Ferdinand Haase. None could speak more than a few halting words of English. At first all went well; the weather was warm and clear and Captain John Williams and his mate, William Lankford of Somerset County, were civil though distant.

A week of squalls kept the *Eva* moored in Crisfield, and when Captain Williams sailed back out on the Bay, he was determined to amass several thousand bushels of oysters to compensate for lost time. The weather turned cold, and the tossing Chesapeake made the Germans seasick. Mayher complained of feeling unwell and told his friends that he had severe pains in his side and was unable to work. Captain Williams, however, was in the middle of a successful oyster run and refused to let him off. When Mayher replied that he was suffering from exposure and could not work, Williams and Lankford knocked him down and beat him severely. From that day on, Mayher was subjected to the most horrible treatment while Boye and Haase were paralyzed with fear. The mate beat him daily with a marlin spike and often kicked him until he fainted. Still refusing to work, Mayher was beaten with a rope until he yelled with pain. To stop his cries the captain planted his foot on the victim's throat and stifled him into unconsciousness. On another occasion the mate hoisted the hapless German up by the halyards, stripped him from the waist down and drenched him with icy water. On the day before his death Otto Mayher was strung up by his thumbs, the body being suspended several feet above the flooring of the boat. Mayher grew so weak that he could scarcely walk, and when the *Eva* reached Lower Fairmount in Somerset County, he was unable to help unload the boat. In a fit of rage, Captain Williams beat the German across the loins with an iron bar and Mayher shrieked on the ground in agony. The unloading continued and Boye and Haase were ordered to bring their unconscious comrade on to the deck. Later that night the two terrified Germans saw Mayher rise from the deck and summon his last ounces of strength to escape from the *Eva*. As he staggered on to the shore again, the captain grabbed him, threw him to the ground and broke his neck.

Following a long whispered conference, Williams and Lankford decided to inform the authorities of Mayher's death. The story that they agreed upon was that the German had fallen into the hold of the vessel and fatally injured himself. Before he died, they said, he must have walked to the shore where he was found. A respected resident of Somerset County, Captain Williams was asked to serve on the coroner's jury in Princess Anne as well as be the principal witness. The jury subsequently found that Mayher died of natural causes, and his body was buried in a shallow trench near the Lower Fairmount wharf and quickly forgotten.

Although Captain Williams treated Boye and Haase much better after the incident, they were afraid for their lives. When the *Eva* discharged a cargo the mate always ordered the Germans below and watched them carefully. Finally, on December 20, Williams, convinced that they could not harm him, released the two men in Crisfield. It was his and his mate's word against theirs. Driven on by what seemed to be the furies of Hell, the two Germans begged and borrowed their way back to Baltimore. When the two haggard and shivering men appeared at the German consulate in rags on December 24, 1884, the consul could hardly believe what he had heard. After a couple of whiskeys and a large hot meal, the men began to regain their composure, and the consul dispatched a messenger to summon his attorney, Louis P. Hennighausen, to record their testimony.

That Christmas Eve as he rode in his carriage to the German consulate on Light Street, Hennighausen clenched his teeth in anger over this latest atrocity involving German immigrants on Chesapeake Bay. A strong-willed and out-spoken maritime lawyer, Hennighausen was an immigrant himself who had risen out of the waterfront slums to a prominent position in Baltimore. As legal counsel to the city's German Society, he was determined to end these abuses and capture Mayher's murderers even if he had to do it with his own money. Hennighausen knew the waterfront, carried a pistol, and feared no one.

Shortly thereafter, Hennighausen and the German Society hired Julius Conrad, a private detective skilled in maritime cases, and dispatched him and the two witnesses, Boye and Haase, to Somerset County to testify against Captain Williams. Another trial was held and this time Captain Williams was convicted of murder in the second degree and sentenced to eighteen years in prison. Tempers grew hot in the Bayside communities of the lower Shore over Williams's conviction, and watermen immediately began to campaign for a governor's pardon for Williams.

A month later a delegation of men from the German Society, the Hibernian Society, and the Baltimore business community traveled to Annapolis to request legislation protecting sailors from tyrannical dredge boat captains. The Maryland General Assembly, however, adjourned without acting on the matter. The oyster interests and county governments opposed any interference by Annapolis, and the politicians were reluctant to incur their wrath. Undaunted, the German Society posted signs in English and German in the waterfront districts of New York, Philadelphia, and Baltimore warning men away from the dredge boats. Hennighausen became a one-man legal machine in his relentless drive to use existing federal and state laws to prohibit kidnapping and slavery on the Chesapeake. The German Society

61

hired its own tug and turned it over to a United States marshal who attempted to rescue Paddies from their captors. In 1886 the marshal and several deputies destroyed several "paddy shacks" on Hoopers Island in Dorchester County. These were prison compounds for shanghaied crewmen and served as a source of free labor for any dredge boat captain who needed an extra hand, willing or unwilling. Gazing at the shivering half-starved men, a reporter for *Harper's* noted that "if the tender-hearted among the oyster consumers knew with how much pain and suffering these bivalves were brought from their salt water homes to the dining table, they would not eat them in the happy frame of mind necessary to a full appreciation of this finest of all seafoods."

Meanwhile the Baltimore newspapers carried stories of "those poor devils" who had been shanghaied by unscrupulous dredgers. In order to avoid giving a captive crew member his due wages, a dredge captain would turn the ship's tiller abruptly and the boom of the sail would swing violently and knock the man overboard into the icy Chesapeake. "Paid off at the boom," many floated ashore and were buried in unmarked graves. Even more than forty years later, Lorie Quinn, a Crisfield newspaper editor, remembered how young men drowned and frozen blue would be found in fishnets in Tangier Sound.

By 1889 the German Society had secured the overwhelming support of the Baltimore civic community, and the legislature yielded to demands for humane treatment of dredge boat crews. The new maritime law of January 1, 1890, required harbor masters and seaport authorities to keep a registry of dredge boat crews and copies of their contracts for time and wages. Further, the new law held dredge captains accountable for every man not returned; those who violated the law risked a six-month prison sentence.

The dredgers, however, defied Annapolis, and in 1892 Governor George Brown dispatched Captain Edward Biddleman, a United States marshal, and Heinrich Tieck, an attorney for the German Society, on the Maryland police boat

Governor McLane to arrest a dredger who had shanghaied fourteen recently arrived immigrants. Tieck was armed with nine writs of habeas corpus and thirteen warrants from the United States District Court. On December 29, 1892, the *McLane* entered the Potomac River, and Marshal Biddleman seized the oyster sloop *Partnership* and arrested Captain Stewart H. Evans and three Negro mates, Walter Sykes, Joseph Sanders, and Andrew Cooper and fined them $200 each. For two months Evans and his crew had held their crew of fourteen captive; when rescued the immigrants were overjoyed and embraced and kissed each other.

Later that week the *McLane* rescued the ice-bound *Viola*, which had been deserted by the captain and his mate. The crew had been left without food or water and would have perished after a few more days as it was over a mile to shore and the water was covered with treacherous ice. In a telegram from Crisfield, Heinrich Tieck reported that about 150 vessels were frozen in and "the suffering among the poor oyster dredgers must be terrible. I still have much evidence of other cases on my hands, the difficulty is that we cannot do anything in Crisfield against the cruel captains but have to apply to the U.S. Court in Baltimore."

The use of the state police boat *McLane* to liberate Paddies drew an angry response from the state oyster industry; the Baltimore Oyster Exchange passed resolutions of protest against Governor Brown and used its political influence to have the law so amended that it became ineffective. The horrible treatment of sailors on the Chesapeake continued into the twentieth century, and even after the passage of the federal Shanghaing Act of 1908 newspapers carried occasional stories of slavery before the mast.

Technological innovation rather than the federal courts put an end to involuntary servitude on Chesapeake Bay. About 1906 oyster dredgers began to get relief from the hand windlass as eight-horsepower gasoline engines for winding in the heavy dredges became available. With power winders four men could do the work that had required eight men in the era of hand winders. The new gasoline winders not only relieved the labor shortage on the Bay but also allowed the boats to obtain more oysters. By the end of 1908 many dredge boat captains had purchased gasoline-powered winders, and the tyranny of the hand windlass soon became only legend on the Bay.

The great scramble for the fast dollar during the oyster boom had weakened the social fabric of many maritime communities in the Chesapeake. In an age that translated the Darwinian struggle in nature into social philosophy, many men in the tidewater resorted to lawlessness and mayhem. A cursory investigation of the Eastern Shore in the late nineteenth century reveals an astonishing record of rape, arson, and murder, and few villages remained immune from the violence that accompanied boom times.

The murder of Captain Frank Cooper on board his oyster sloop *James V. Daiger* in the harbor at Deal's Island on June 16, 1893, created intense excitement throughout the state of Maryland. A native of Carter's Creek, Virginia, Cooper had operated a flourishing freight business in oysters and farm produce and was well known along the rivers of the lower Eastern Shore. When authorities found his decomposed body floating in the harbor, they immediately sent out a search party to arrest his two black crewmen, Henry Taylor and Arthur Courtney. On the following day the two blacks were apprehended in Irvington, Virginia, as they attempted to hire on a schooner bound for Baltimore. While the two men waited in jail at Lancaster Court House, an angry mob led by Cooper's widow assembled outside. Courtney was terrified by the prospect of being lynched and quickly confessed the crime to the posse from Somerset County.

For several months Courtney and Taylor had worked for Captain Cooper as deck hands and oyster crew. Although the captain had a very good year with his freighting business, he quarreled incessantly with the two Negroes over money. The blacks demanded better wages and accused Cooper of reneging on earlier promises that he had made to them. Cooper also had most of their clothes and personal belongings locked in his cabin to prevent them from leaving.

One Sunday when Cooper came up on deck, the two blacks were outraged upon seeing that the captain was wearing Courtney's white linen suit. "This is my suit now," Cooper said gruffly. "And if you don't like the way things are run on this boat, go ashore and hire on with somebody else." Later that night Courtney and Taylor resolved to murder Cooper and take his money to settle their grudge against him. The captain went to bed at nine o'clock, and the Negroes waited until he was sound asleep before attacking him with a lead pipe. Taylor's blow glanced off Cooper's head and he sprang up immediately.

"Oh, boys, if you will not hurt me, I will give you fifty dollars," the captain pleaded.

The two blacks, momentarily caught off guard by the offer, glanced at each other in the dim kerosene light. "We have started it," Taylor growled. "If he lives we will have to go to the penitentiary, and we may as well finish it!" Taylor grabbed the captain and Courtney struck him with the pipe. As he struck, Cooper threw up his left arm and warded off the blow and escaped their grasp. Panic-stricken and bleeding, Cooper ran up the steps to the deck and started to yell for help from the other boats in the harbor. Taylor grabbed a quilt, threw it over Cooper's head and wrestled him to the deck. This time Courtney struck him with a handspike. In their desperate struggle, Cooper fell overboard; as he thrashed in the water, the two blacks jumped into the yawl boat and smashed in his skull with an oar. In a few seconds Cooper's lifeless body sank to the bottom. The murderers then went to the captain's cabin, broke into his closet, and found his big leather pocketbook containing $55. The two men then searched Cooper's clothing for jewelry and change. Then they lit a globe lamp and began to wash the blood stains off the cabin floor and deck and afterwards went to sleep.

The enormity of the crime did not disturb Arthur Courtney's conscience until he awakened in the morning. Gazing across the water at Deal's Island, he knew that it would take more than strength to avoid a hangman's noose in this white community.

"Don't worry," Taylor said. "We'll tell everyone ashore that the captain has left us on the boat without paying us our wages and we'll file a claim with the harbor master for our back pay. That will look like we haven't done anything wrong. Then we'll go and tell Cooper's wife that he has deserted us and ask for his whereabouts. Swear on it that we will hang before we tell." That hanging was to occur much sooner than Taylor thought.

When the Baltimore *Sun* learned of the Cooper murder, the newspaper dispatched its crack reporter, Thomas J. Ewell, to the Eastern Shore, and a day after the Negroes' apprehension the reporter arrived at Irvington. The *Sun* had warned Ewell that the crowd in the village would be in an ugly mood, and the reporter carried a Colt revolver in his pocket. Ewell contacted the sheriff of Somerset County and offered his assistance in transporting the Negroes back to Maryland. The next morning when Sheriff Frank Tull and his men took the blacks from the jail, Cooper's widow began to scream, "They killed my Frank!" and the mob rushed the sheriff's carriage. Sheriff Tull stood up in the carriage, put his whip to the horses, and arrived at Carter's Creek Landing to board the steamer *Joppa* minutes ahead of the lynchers.

"Boys, hide for your lives," Tull yelled as he forced the blacks into a cargo hold and placed himself on top of the hatch. Before the steamer could leave the wharf, a group of about twenty men jumped on board the boat in pursuit of the Negroes.

"Rush him!" yelled the crowd, and the men knocked Tull off the hatch and brought up the two terrified blacks. Suddenly a pistol shot rang out and one of the mobsmen fell bleeding to the floor. Tull charged up to the balcony and cut the rope that had already been placed around Courtney's neck. From his vantage point on the upper deck, Ewell kept his pistol trained on the crowd. "There won't be any lynching on the *Joppa* today," he warned. "We are taking these boys back to Princess Anne and the next man to come forward will be shot dead!"

Before the week was over, Courtney and Taylor were taken to Princess Anne and tried. The jury rendered a guilty verdict and Judge Henry Page sentenced the two young blacks to death by hanging in December. Throughout the trial the jail had been besieged by visitors, and Courtney and Taylor joked with friends and strangers. A group of black Virginia watermen handed the two convicted Negroes a package containing two white linen shirts and two black cravats. "You boys is still oystermen," said a Virginian, "and we want you to be dressed fancy and proud when you go on out." The two men spent their last night cracking jokes and laughing about their approaching doom. Neither slept during his last night in jail. At dawn on the morning of the hanging, the jail guards brought them each a pint of stewed oysters, coffee, bread, and butter. Later they were unchained and allowed to bathe and dress.

Outside a huge crowd had knocked down the fence that had been erected around the gallows to prevent a public viewing of the execution. "Ain't no fence gonna keep us from watching this!" yelled a determined spectator, and several men ripped away the fence boards. Ultimately two thousand men and women witnessed the hanging. They were packed dozens deep around the scaffold; they were perched on the fence surrounding the jail; they climbed neighboring trees in their desire to watch the proceedings; and they climbed roofs of houses overlooking the jail and perched themselves on chimney tops. At 11:45 A.M. on December 15, 1893, Henry Taylor, aged nineteen, and Arthur Courtney, aged twenty-four, were hanged. Thirty minutes later, they were cut down, pronounced dead, and turned over to a black undertaker for burial. A large well-dressed group of dredge boat captains from Deal's Island had watched the hanging, secure in its belief that justice had been done.

The murders of Captain Frank Cooper and Otto Mayher were merely highlights of a theme of violence that prevailed on Chesapeake Bay. Journalists who covered this turbulent region for *Harper's, Scribner's Magazine,* and the Baltimore *Sun* often referred to oystermen as "water Arabs." Just as the Arabs of the Sahara had profited enormously from slavery and disrupted the African continent, so did the slaving dredgers disrupt the Chesapeake in pursuit of the oyster. In Arab life roaming bands of nomads made their own law on the desert; the same state of affairs prevailed on the Bay.

Throughout the Chesapeake, watermen bowed obsequiously to H. C. Rowe, the powerful oyster pasha who controlled the fate of thousands with the ease and ruthlessness of an Ottoman prince. In an age of economic growth, business strife, and great fortunes, H. C. Rowe was the giant of the American oyster industry. Starting modestly as the inheritor of a bankrupt oyster-packing house in Connecticut in 1858, Rowe allied himself with the new oyster farmers of Long Island Sound who were attempting to reseed the exhausted beds and revive the industry. After the Civil War, Rowe learned that the oyster beds of France and England had become diseased and exhausted and that fish merchants in London were willing to pay fifty dollars a bushel for oysters. The American sensed that he could make a financial killing as a trans-Atlantic oyster wholesaler, and in the fall of 1871 Rowe mortgaged his business and borrowed twenty thousand dollars from several banks in New Haven to purchase the *Salsette,* a small ocean-going steamer that could carry five thousand bushels of oysters. That winter Rowe signed contracts with Nelson and Tull and Company and the Riggin Brothers, two Crisfield packing firms, for three thousand bushels of oysters. On February 16, 1872, the heavily laden *Salsette* steamed down the Chesapeake, bound for London.

The *Salsette*'s cargo was the gamble of a lifetime, as Rowe could get very little insurance to cover the ship's risky trans-

Atlantic voyage. The boat suffered several breakdowns at sea and only the severe Atlantic weather kept the cargo from spoiling. On March 8, Rowe dashed to the telegraph office in New Haven to learn that the oysters had sold on the London market for thirty dollars a bushel. Almost overnight an obscure Long Island Sound oyster packer had become a wealthy man. With his fortune assured, the Connecticut oyster speculator bought another ship, a steamer with six dredges with a capacity for raking in eight thousand bushels of oysters a day in water forty deet deep. In November 1880, the behemoth dredge *H. C. Rowe and Company* sailed from New York for Baltimore; its arrival on the Chesapeake signaled that Rowe was now determined to be a major force in the Maryland oyster industry.

Every year nearly five million bushels of oysters were sold in Baltimore, and after 1880 a large share of this harvest would be controlled by Rowe and his Maryland business associates. Through bribery, forged licenses, and copartnerships with Maryland residents, Rowe evaded the state residency requirement and controlled an oyster fleet of nearly one hundred sailing vessels and seven hundred seamen. In his well-fitted and luxurious "lay boat" Rowe met daily with saloon keepers, oyster dealers, and trans-Atlantic shippers, entertaining them with chorus girls and generous amounts of whiskey. When his own men could not provide him with oysters, Rowe bought them from pirates and renegades. Thus with the additional stimulus of H. C. Rowe and Company and the foreign trade, the local price of oysters skyrocketed during the 1880s.

The net effect of the boom at home and abroad, complained the *Baltimore American*, was that "by far the greater proportion of the oysters brought to Baltimore are caught at night, on Sundays, and on forbidden grounds." Although in 1872 the state had passed a culling law that prohibited the harvesting of oysters less than two-and-one-half inches from hinge to mouth, it was widely disregarded. Oyster brokers were anxious to buy every oyster they could get and would export oysters to the antipodes if they could turn a dollar. Baltimore's frenzied waterfront commerce was sustained by romantic stories of self-made men who gained fortunes from the oyster trade. Said one Baltimore official, "Instances occur of vessels clearing from fifteen to seventeen thousand dollars on a single trip from our waters to New England." In both Crisfield and Baltimore oyster boats were jammed in the harbors so tightly that a man could walk across the water from one end of the slips to the other. "The oyster craze has taken hold of Baltimore," wrote one visitor to the city in 1885, and rumors of dwindling harvests only intensified the struggles of the watermen. With the largely defunct Oyster Navy unable to curb bloodshed on the Bay, the Maryland oyster industry entered one of its most violent periods. Until General Joseph B. Seth and several well-equipped gunboats restored order in 1888, neither sportsmen, commercial vessels, nor steamboat passengers were safe on the turbulent waters of the Chesapeake.

JAMES E. STANSBURY,
OYSTER, FRUIT AND VEGETABLE PACKER,
AND SHELL-LIME KILNS.
Atlantic Wharf, near Boston Street, Canton,   BALTIMORE.

Chapter 4

HELL ON THE HALF-SHELL

I N LATE AUGUST 1885 there was a feeling of expectancy in the air as watermen carried their long wooden and steel tongs down to the docks and the blacksmith shops for repair and began to refurbish their boats for the grueling winter oyster season. The gossip in barber shops, saloons, and grocery stores centered on oysters, oyster rakes, dredgers, possible prices per bushel, and weather conditions. "There is a passionate interest of oystermen in their trade," wrote one observer. "Everything to do with oysters, from tonging to marketing, is, to them, a subject of the most vivid and eternal freshness." With the advent of oyster season bayside hamlets like Rock Hall and St. Michaels sprang to life from the dreamy slumber of the summer months.

In Crisfield William Gibson strode quickly along the docks toward his oyster-packing house. William Gibson and Company expected an exceptionally good season, even though Tangier Sound was not as productive as in former times. "Thar's plenty arsters left up in the rivers," piped Jimmy Tull, Gibson's friend and fellow packer, "and them drudgers'll git em!" Crisfield packers, while often imperious toward the small-scale tongers, courted the dredge boat captains as if they were imperial potentates. With over four hundred thousand bushels of oysters coming into Crisfield annually, it did not pay to antagonize those who brought in the major share of the harvest. The streets and docks of Crisfield were lined with offices and warehouses, and their signs—Crockett and Riggin, J. Sterling and Company,

THE OYSTER WARS

William Evans, Church and Stubs, William Gibson and Co., A. B. Riggin, James S. Tull Co., Nelson and Tull, Long Coulbourn and Co.—served as a guide to the town's wealth and power.

The riverfront towns of the Eastern Shore also looked forward to sharing the largesse of the almighty oyster. On Saturday night many watermen would sail up the Chester River to Chestertown for a rowdy evening of beery celebration at the Odd Fellows, Knights of Pythias, or any of the other lodges that provided Kent County with much of its social life. Further south on the Pocomoke River, Newtown, not yet accustomed to its new name of Pocomoke City, was a well-known gambling den for watermen. Despite the preaching of the Methodist church and the Anti-Saloon League against liquor, Newtown's general stores supplied watermen with ample stocks of whiskey. Every store counter had its "pint and pitcher," and customers were invited to step up and take a free drink. "Well, gentlemen," went the familiar toast, "here's good and plenty." Superstitious watermen also frequented Newtown's fortunetellers and conjurers. In the Wicomico River area the village of Whitehaven was a busy place. It contained a fishing fleet, a good-sized shipyard, and popular grog shops famous for good cheap rum that had been brought up on Chesapeake lumber boats from the Caribbean.

Many of these river towns were the homes of black watermen who held positions of leadership in their communities and worked on steamboats in the summer season. These men were considered the aristocrats of the Eastern Shore Negro community and were fierce champions of black rights. One such black oysterman was Edward Wilson of Somerset County. Born in 1852 of free parents, this mulatto oysterman served as a power broker between whites and blacks in the county and guaranteed the black vote in hotly contested elections. Wilson supervised black patronage matters in Somerset for the state Republican organization for over thirty years and was subsequently rewarded by President William McKinley in 1897 with a sinecure in the Baltimore Customs House.

Thus it was not surprising that in the autumn of 1885 a delegation of black watermen visited Captain Wilson at his home in Upper Fairmount. Unless he helped them, the watermen implored, the oyster pirates would force them out of the Manokin and Wicomico rivers and they would soon starve. White tongers were equally desperate, and within a short time Wilson had both groups building fortifications on shore near the oyster bars. The next step, Wilson decided, was to bring the war home to the enemy; in November he and his men captured the oyster dredge *Florence* and burned her to the water line. Later Captain Wilson and his band of oystermen placed a cannon on land to bombard the pirate vessels when they invaded the Wicomico.

In January 1886 the oystermen of Somerset summoned the police boat *Kent* to arrest the pirate dredgers, and a fierce battle ensued that resulted in the death of several men. After excessive gunfire the pirates escaped in a fog. Although Wilson and his men remained watchful and a police sloop continued to patrol the oyster grounds near the mouths of the Wicomico and Nanticoke rivers, the pirates often returned at night, their sails smeared with mud to escape detection in the moonlight, and looted the beds of hundreds of bushels of oysters. Both Maryland police boats and Somerset's vigilante watermen, boasted the pirates, were about as annoying as green-headed flies.

In the 1880s the Chester River oyster beds were one of the greatest natural treasures of the Bay country. Local watermen harvested thousands of bushels annually from its waters, and Kent County prospered. Over one hundred tongers worked at the mouth of the Chester River; in the distance the men looked as if they were walking on stilts. With the rapid depletion of the beds out in the Bay, though, it was not long before the pirate dredgers invaded the Chester and the crack of Winchesters resounded across the water.

THE OYSTER WARS

Under cover of a thick fog on March 18, 1881, a fleet of oyster dredges passed inside the headlands of the Chester River and started taking oysters from grounds legally reserved for the tongers. Several dredgers ran down and capsized tongers in the river. The pirate sloop *Eugene*, commanded by Captain John Wilson and owned by a Baltimore oyster packer, was heavily armed. When the police schooner *Nannie Merryman* entered the river, she hailed the *Eugene* to heave to for boarding. The *Eugene* replied with a broadside of shotgun fire. Using its swivel Hotchkiss rifle, the *Merryman* happily poured lead into the *Eugene* and the other dredge boats and captured the *Merrick* and the *Kite*, both Baltimore vessels. Much to his annoyance, Fred Bucheimer, the ships' owner, was summoned to Chestertown and fined two hundred dollars for illegal dredging.

The swift response of the *Merryman* to pirates on the Chester River was indicative of new leadership in the Maryland Oyster Navy in the late 1880s. James F. Maddell, its commander, kept his flotilla of three steamers and ten schooners out on the Bay 150 days a year. Although the state only budgeted three thousand dollars annually, Maddell was able to maintain his force through fines and license fees; and despite its many problems, the Oyster Navy this time was welcomed on the rivers of the Eastern Shore by the harassed and angry tongers. Despite the Navy's lack of equipment and trained manpower, one seasoned observer noted that if the force were disbanded, "in a few weeks the Bay would be in a state of anarchy." The main problem confronting the oyster police boats that patrolled the Chester River area was that they were desperately short of guns and ammunition. "It is useless," wrote Deputy Commander William T. George, "to attempt the arrest of a large fleet without a cannon on board." Also, seven hundred well-manned, fast-sailing oyster dredges scattered over such a large area as the Chesapeake Bay were difficult to watch, especially at night. Thus the problems that Hunter Davidson had identified in 1868 continued to haunt the Oyster Navy two decades later. To make

Above, Pirates attack the *Julia Hamilton*, *Harper's Weekly*, March 1, 1884.
Below, The capture of a pirate, *Harper's Weekly*, March 1, 1884.

matters worse, the Chester River attracted Gus Rice, one of the most formidable of the Chesapeake's oyster desperadoes.

Gus Rice often bragged that it took a special kind of man to survive on the Eastern Shore. There had been times when he was so broke that he picked peaches in local orchards at thirty cents a day. In the years after the Civil War he had been a drifter, a barroom brawler, and a waterman. Living by his wits and his fists, Rice had been hired as captain of the *J. C. Mahoney*, a pungy boat owned by a Baltimore oyster speculator, and was the acknowledged leader of the oyster pirates of Chester River. Captain Rice was a dilapidated specimen in foul-weather clothing and a battered waterproof hat. His purple-red weathered face was well known in the saloons of Crisfield and Baltimore, and his rough growth of beard made him look every inch the killer he was. He vowed that no man would prevent him from catching oysters, and many people remembered how years earlier Gus Rice had plotted to murder Hunter Davidson.

Gus Rice recruited his men from the docks of Baltimore and the jails of the Eastern Shore. The latter Rice knew at first hand because he had experienced more than his share of trouble with the law. During the late nineteenth century, impoverished homeless men were not welcomed in the tightly knit communities of the Eastern Shore. In Cambridge and Easton the public whipping post and pillory were familiar sights, and oyster pirates like Rice often claimed that the humiliating and painful whip called "the Sheriff's Cat" caused more dread in watermen than any peril on the Bay. After serving a harsh thirty-day sentence building dusty roads out of oyster shells for crimes of vagrancy and drunkenness, many drifters followed the water. Aboard an oyster boat on Chesapeake Bay a man did not have to fear county commissioners and stern judges. Outcasts from the farm communities of the Shore, these poor and desperate men gathered at Oxford and Crisfield in rough camaraderie that transcended racial lines. Destiny awaited them when they joined Gus Rice's pirate band.

Meanwhile, in the harbor at Annapolis, Captain William T. George exercised every morning with his Indian clubs on the deck of his police sloop *Helen M. Baughman*. It was one way to get the circulation up and the mind alert. For two seasons Gus Rice had eluded him, George frequently complained, because of the "inefficiency of the force, the leniency of the courts and hair-splitting lawyers." The *Baughman's* crew of four had only a hundred rounds of ammunition between them, and the men were reluctant to fight the pirates. Also Captain George noted apprehensively, a wooden sloop would sink in the icy waters of the Chester if rammed by a pirate dredge.

In the winter of 1887 the oyster police, despite Commander Maddell's enthusiasm and industry, were no match for the pirates, and Gus Rice and his flotilla raided the Chester River beds with impunity. The pirates' strategy was shrewd and simple. The dredges only worked on moonlit nights, and to avoid being surprised they stationed a sentinel boat at the mouth of the Chester. At the top of the sentinel's mast the pirates placed a globe light, which was lowered when the oyster police were sighted and hoisted to signal the approach of an enemy. During the day the sentinel boat used a flag. All members of the pirate dredge fleet contributed a fixed number of bushels of oysters to compensate the sentinel boat for its labors. At this time, observed the Baltimore *Sun*, there were two classes of oyster pirates. One class worked until the police appeared and then fled, while the other class made war on the police boats and drove them off. In the Chester River, with a fortune in oysters at stake, the pirate dredgers were so accustomed to fighting police and tongers that they had iron shields placed around the wheel to protect the dredging skipper.

By the early spring of 1888 the tongers of Chester River grew so desperate that they mounted a pair of cannon on the shore and attempted to drive the dredge boats away. The watermen, however, were so inept that they were incapable of hitting anything with their one-pounders. While the *J. C.*

Mahoney and the other pirate vessels ignored the cannon at first, they later decided to give the Chester watermen a few merry lessons in warfare. One April night after an exceptionally good haul of oysters, Gus Rice broke out a few jugs of whiskey for his compatriots, and soon the dozen men on board decided to send a raiding party ashore. When they came upon the fortress containing the cannon, they found only a single watchman huddled in the shed against the cold night air. Gus Rice was so amused at the tongers' ineptitude that he ordered the watchman stripped of his clothing, and the naked and terrified man was sent to Kent and Queen Anne's counties with a message: it would take more than two one-pounders and a sleeping watchman to keep Gus Rice out of the Chester River. Rice's men then loaded the cannon on the *J. C. Mahoney* and sped off before dawn.

Finally the enraged Kent countians put so much pressure on the state legislature that Annapolis dispatched the *Helen M. Baughman* to the Chester River. The *Baughman* focused its attention on the *Kite*, a pirate vessel that had been separated from the other dredgers. After several wide misses with her newly installed howitzer, the *Baughman* finally made a lucky shot and dismasted the *Kite*. Pulling alongside the crippled vessel, Captain George opened fire with his shotgun, and the frightened pirates quickly surrendered. All the dredgers were placed in irons. After nearly two years of frustrating chases, Captain George had met and overwhelmed his quarry. Later, at their trial, the captured dredgers reported that the crew members of the police boat were so delighted with their prowess that they were all hilariously drunk by the time they reached port at Chestertown.

Gus Rice, however, continued to remain a law unto himself until one night when he made a costly mistake. Sighting a ship in a fog that looked like an oyster police steamer, Gus Rice ordered his men to fire on it. The pirates were excellent marksmen, and their bullets whined and crashed through the steamer's cabins. Unfortunately for the pirates, the craft was not a police boat but an innocent passenger vessel, the *Cor-*

sica, a steamboat owned by the Baltimore and Eastern Shore
Line. On board the *Corsica* were many women and children
who had feared for their lives as the storm of bullets hit the
vessel.

The *Corsica* incident sparked widespread indignation in
the state, and Baltimore and Annapolis newspapers demanded an end to Gus Rice and his pirate band. When the
Bay police received the order from the governor's office to
proceed to the Chester, the *Governor McLane*, the flagship
steamer of the Oyster Navy, was in Annapolis having a
twelve-pound howitzer placed on the deck. While the car-
penters remained on board furiously working to complete
the howitzer installation, Captain Thomas C. B. Howard
loaded extra men and rifles and hurried across the Bay.

Howard had joined the Oyster Navy in 1887 and had
quickly earned a reputation as a quick-witted policeman on
the Bay. A Dorchester County native whose family had
fished and tonged oysters in the rivers of the Eastern Shore
for generations, Howard, noted *Harper's*, "violated the prece-
dents of years by daring to think that it was his duty to
enforce the laws." At first the dredgers ignored him, but after
several confrontations with the *McLane* the Annapolis jail
was filled with Howard's prisoners. Howard's mate, Oliver
Crowder of St. Mary's County, had attached armor halfway
up the pilot house, and when the police boat went into battle,
Crowder removed the compass from the binnacle and piloted
the *McLane* while sitting on the floor behind the armor.

As night descended on December 10, 1888, Howard took
his telescope and scouted the situation before moving into
the Chester River. About seventy dredgers were busily at
work. The captain and two of his men were lowered in a skiff,
and in the darkness Howard and his men rowed over to a
dredge boat at anchor. In an instant Howard surprised the
pirate captain, dropped the boat's sails, and arrested the crew.
Within an hour he had captured another dredge in a similar
fashion before the rest of the pirate fleet became alarmed.
Returning to the *McLane*, Howard surged up the Chester

after more dredgers. As the wind was blowing downstream, the dredges were tacking back and forth across the bow of the *McLane* and made easy targets for the steamer's howitzer.

Gus Rice, though, had planned for the oyster police. Out of the darkness lurched a giant raft of twelve dredge boats lashed together with chain and drifting rapidly before the wind and a strong current. Above deck the raft was fortified with large iron plates. Suddenly Gus Rice cried out, "Join me boys in victory or in Hell," and thirty yelling pirates began to fire on the *McLane*. In response Howard ordered his assistant engineer to fire the howitzer, and the *McLane* discharged four shots. Each shot passed through the rigging of the rafted boats, as the *McLane* was too close to depress the howitzer to hit the hulls. When the steamer passed the raft, Howard and his men peppered the dredges with rifle fire.

The raft, however, was so well fortified that neither rifle fire nor the howitzer had any effect on the pirates. "Come about 180 degrees, Mr. Crowder," thundered Captain Howard. "Full speed ahead!" The *McLane* crashed dead center into the raft with the pirate vessel *Julia H. Jones* taking the brunt. One of her crew leaped to safety aboard the *McLane* and was taken prisoner. Other above-deck crewmen jumped to the dredge boats tied alongside.

The police steamer, meanwhile, was caught in a deadly cross fire, and the mate at the howitzer was severely wounded. With Crowder still at the wheel, Howard ordered the *McLane* taken astern, halted, then full speed ahead, this time into the dredger *J. C. Mahoney*. The oyster police now returned a deadly fire with their Winchesters, and the last of the pirates panicked, cast off their lines, and scattered. The *Jones* and the *Mahoney* sank quickly. Unknown to the oyster police, shanghaied crewmen had been locked in the forepeaks of both vessels. As the boats went under, the imprisoned men pounded futilely on the battened hatches.

At the battle's end the *McLane* had sunk two vessels, captured two more, and had taken over a dozen prisoners.

Above, Police steamer *McLane*. Courtesy: Enoch Pratt Library, Baltimore.
Below, Police powerboat *Venus*. Courtesy: The Baltimore *Sun*.

Several dredge boat captains had escaped, including the wily oyster pirate, Gus Rice. The police were unable to determine how many Paddies and dredgers had drowned. Several days later the *McLane* was joined by another police steamer, the *Governor Thomas*, and the two vessels moved southward to Eastern Bay to confront the pirate dredgers. With their defeat in the battle of Chester River still fresh in their minds, several dredgers beached their boats and ran. Afterwards Captain Howard made a triumphant return to Annapolis and was given a hero's welcome by the state legislature. Politicians and visitors were invited to board the *McLane* and marveled at Howard's rack of polished rifles in the cabin and the lean-jacketed twelve-pounder in the bow of the powerful tug. Howard would remain active in the Oyster Navy until after the turn of the century, and when his quick eye failed to detect upon the mainsail of any craft the license number in large black Arabic numerals, Howard hailed the offending shipmaster. "Captain, where's your license number?" he demanded. Sometimes Howard could be seen on the *McLane* with two or three delinquent boats in tow. Unfortunately, the *McLane* could not be everywhere; and while law and order had been imposed on the Chester, hell flourished on the half-shell in the Little Choptank River and the waters of the Potomac.

On November 8, 1888, the police sloop *Eliza Hayward* hailed fourteen pirate dredgers working in the Little Choptank River and fired upon them with its cannon when the vessels failed to respond. The pirate schooners quickly surrounded the *Hayward*, and two dozen riflemen blasted her before the police sloop fled to Oxford. The captain and the crew refused to take the *Hayward* out again. Oyster dredgers, the men of the *Hayward* learned to their surprise, had only contempt for the state naval militia. Although the steamer *McLane* visited the Little Choptank shortly thereafter, about fifty dredge boats of all sizes, rigs, and classes appeared in the river following the tug's departure.

HELL ON THE HALF-SHELL

On January 12, 1889, another police boat, the *E. B. Groome*, accosted the pirates, and a bitter gun fight ensued. The *Groome* ran out of ammunition and was forced to withdraw; as the police boat sailed away, the dredgers announced their victory with blowing horns and Indian war cries. The battle had lasted more than two hours, during which time over a thousand rounds were fired. Later the *Groome*'s first mate, Charles B. Cator, reported that bullets had penetrated the police boat's hull, cut the rigging, and perforated the sails. The dredgers, he said, had been eager to fight, and "seeing how utterly powerless we were to cope with so many boats, each of which appeared to be better armed than our own vessel, we retreated, leaving the dredgers in possession of the ground." Police authority on the Little Choptank was rapidly degenerating into farce.

Among those wounded during the battle was James Castus, the hard-fighting Negro first mate of the Virginia dredge boat *T. B. Schall*, and his fellow pirates vowed revenge. Under the cover of darkness fourteen dredgers boarded the *E. B. Groome* at Cambridge and surprised the police. Armed with shotguns, pistols, and axes, the outlaws compelled Captain Charles W. Frazier and his crew to get the sloop under way. Disarmed and ashamed, the crew members were forced to accompany the pirates back to the main anchorage of the dredging fleet. The shanghaied oyster police were put to work at the windlass and after several exhausting days were allowed to row home in a small skiff. The *E. B. Groome* was later found many miles down the Bay stripped of its rigging and abandoned.

The pirates, complained Dorchester watermen, were stealing tens of thousands of bushels of oysters a day from the Little Choptank. To their regret, it always seemed that the armored police steamer arrived after the dredgers had stripped the beds and moved elsewhere. Periodically the oyster pirates terrorized the local population. When the citizens of Cambridge organized a militia to protect the oyster bars of James Island, the dredgers fired on the town and threatened to burn it if Cambridge sent its militia out again. The dredgers, said Sheriff John Marshall of the Dorchester County Oyster Militia, "seem more determined to carry their point this winter than ever before. The oysters are scarce in the Bay and they seemed determined to get the oysters from the rivers at any risk." Outraged by the turn of events on the Little Choptank, Cambridge officials sent a telegram to Annapolis demanding the intervention of the *McLane*. Unlike the case of the Chester River and its emotion-filled *Corsica* incident, the armored police steamers would not come to the rescue. They were locked in a bloody contest that would decide not only the fate of the oyster resources of the Potomac River but the boundaries of Maryland and Virginia as well. Thus Dorchester County stood helpless as the pirate dredge fleet looted the Choptank of its final large cache of oysters and sailed away.

By 1889 increasing concern over diminishing oyster harvests had prompted the Virginia legislature to allow the private leasing of "oyster flats" in the hope that the beds would be replenished by industrious watermen. This policy sparked considerable controversy in those parts of the Chesapeake Bay over which both Virginia and Maryland claimed sovereignty. Hog Island was one such area. Located near the mouth of the Potomac, Hog Island contained several oyster beds which had been leased to Charles R. Lewis, an Onancock, Virginia, oyster dealer. From the outset Lewis had difficulty protecting his grounds from enterprising Maryland watermen because Governor Elihu Jackson had issued a proclamation in Annapolis declaring Hog Island to be the common property of Maryland and Virginia. Oyster leases, argued watermen from nearby Smith Island, were worthless in Maryland, and they regularly looted the Hog Island flats. In Onancock the exasperated Lewis hired Captain William F. Russell, an experienced waterman and deputy of the Virginia oyster militia, and gave him command of the *Ida Augusta*, a steam-powered tug. "If them damned Smith Islanders try to loot my oyster beds," Lewis fumed at Captain Russell, "then sink their vessels!"

On November 27, 1889, the *Ida Augusta* steamed out of Onancock and headed across the Bay to the Potomac River. Around 1:30 in the afternoon the tug swung around Hog Island and Captain Russell began to inspect the Lewis reservation. Off buoy #5 Captain Russell spied the *Lawson*, a Smith Island oyster schooner dredging inside the reserve grounds. George Evans and Henry Lawson were busily hauling in their oyster dredge and scarcely noticed the *Ida Augusta*. Suddenly one of the cullers on the *Lawson* yelled out, "By Jesus she's fixin' to ram us!" The tug crashed into the schooner at mid-ships. The blow was a glancing one and only broke the ship's dredge roller.

"What in the Hell are you doing?" hollered Captain Evans.

There was no reply from Captain Russell, who steered the tug off, and, making for the schooner a second time, crashed through the ship's hull. The schooner listed to starboard and quickly began to sink. Captain Russell then invited the *Lawson*'s crew to get into its yawl boat and board the tug. When Evans and his men boarded the *Ida Augusta*, they saw that the Virginians were well armed and would tolerate no misconduct.

"You just sank a schooner that was worth $1,500 and not insured," sputtered Evans. "Besides the loss of our boat there was $60 in my trunk which was on board." Shaking his fist angrily at Captain Russell, Evans noted, "We shall look to Mr. Lewis for payment of our boat!" As the tug churned its way back to Onancock, the two crews argued heatedly over whether or not Governor Jackson's proclamation gave watermen from Maryland the right to dredge leased beds off Hog Island.

Charles Lewis was waiting on the dock, and his blood rose when he learned what had happened. "Captain Russell was acting on my orders," he told the sullen Marylanders. Looking sternly at the men, Lewis patted the revolver in his belt. "I'll submit to a decision on those beds made by Virginia, but I fail to see what authority Governor Jackson has to issue a proclamation which will allow Maryland boats to make raids on my grounds. No governor of Maryland can issue a proclamation by which I will be robbed," he said.

The Smith Islanders left the following day. "We'll be back on Hog Island someday soon," said Captain Evans. "The next time we will be well-armed and if any one tries to take our boat, we will open fire." Later that month when Captain Russell attempted to seize and board a Maryland dredge boat, the *Ida Augusta* received an unwelcome baptism of bullets. Neither Richmond nor Annapolis seemed inclined or able to curb violence on the Potomac River, and in the winter of 1889 a dozen men died on the Hog Island flats.

A year later the Virginia legislature appointed Captain George Hinman commander of the Virginia flotilla of four armed vessels and specifically charged him with the task of keeping illegal dredgers out of Virginia's waters. As hostilities involving watermen from the two states increased, the Richmond legislature vowed swift punishment of illegal dredgers and passed a law that called for prison sentences of one to three years and loss of their vessel, with half of the proceeds going to the person making the capture of the dredge boat. The Maryland legislature in turn increased appropriations for its oyster police and on August 26, 1891, appointed Joseph B. Seth commander of the newly reorganized Maryland naval militia. Seth, a major shareholder in the Eastern Shore Railroad with extensive business interests in Crisfield, enthusiastically took the force of 130 able-bodied seamen in hand. Both oyster navies, however, chose to argue with one another rather than chase oyster pirates. Finally, in February 1894, the fighting on the Annemessex became so intense that the governor of Maryland dispatched both the *McLane* and the *Governor Thomas* to the scene. The steamers, after warning the dredgers to heave to, fired several salvoes from their cannon and disabled several sloops. Shortly thereafter, the *McLane* was stationed in the Potomac to protect Maryland watermen.

By March 1894, the conflict between the two states and their watermen had become so heated that communication between the two capitals ceased. Lawyers for Annapolis and Richmond quarreled over boundary lines and treaty interpretations and prepared legal briefs that would have delighted the Jesuit fathers. Meanwhile the oyster beds of the Potomac and Chesapeake Bay were being rapidly exhausted. The annual harvest of oysters plummeted from 15,000,000 bushels in 1884 to 9,945,000 in 1889 and decreased significantly every year thereafter. Oysters were being harvested to the point where the reproductive capacity of the oyster beds was greatly diminished. As many beds were not reseeded with oyster shells, the remaining oysters were smothered by the encroaching silt. From Annapolis to Crisfield a new age was dawning on the Chesapeake as the oyster industry began to feel the sting of hard times.

Chapter 5

HARD TIMES

"THE CHESAPEAKE is going to be flat broke if the oysters give out," reflected Dr. William K. Brooks as he hurried his horse-drawn phaeton south on the dirt highway from Baltimore toward Annapolis. "I just hope that the Oyster Commission will do something this time to save the beds." In March 1892 Dr. Brooks knew more about the Chesapeake Bay oyster fishery than any other man in the country. Director of the Chesapeake Zoological Laboratory and professor of biology at Johns Hopkins University, Brooks had participated in several surveys of the oyster beds of the Bay sponsored by the Oyster Commission; his cluttered office was a storehouse of information on shellfish research and production in America, Europe, and Asia. Brooks's study, *The Oyster: A Popular Summary of a Scientific Study*, had been widely acclaimed in Maryland, and he was pleased that so many of the state's political figures had read it and wanted him to testify before the Oyster Commission. Well dressed and handsome despite his owlish eyeglasses, Brooks was eager to meet the Annapolis legislators. Later that week in the state capital Brooks warned the legislature of the impending crisis. "No one in the state took serious steps to regulate the industry when Lieutenant Winslow completed his survey of Tangier Sound," he said. "The oyster laws are not enforced and the Bay is losing its young oysters. Soon there will be none left to replenish the beds." Pausing briefly to look up at the assembled legislators, Brooks warned, "Unless prompt and decisive action is taken, the Chesapeake will go into serious decline."

HARD TIMES

By 1890, said Brooks, the improvements in boats and oyster processing as well as the continued demand for oysters had enormously increased the number of watermen on the Bay. Thus with so many dredgers and tongers, profits in Maryland's oyster industry were spread thin, and watermen, hard-pressed to pay for expensive boats and equipment, were taking up young oysters less than three inches long in order to make ends meet. Also, Brooks reported, the widespread use of oyster shells in lime kilns and fertilizer plants prevented reseeding of the beds. Finally, the most depressing fact confronting the industry was that the annual oyster harvest had decreased from fifteen million bushels in 1884 to slightly less than ten million in 1890.

For over two decades the Chesapeake produced 40 percent of the world's oysters; in 1891 there were 32,104 persons directly engaged in the industry in Maryland. Of these, 28,811 were tongers and dredgers, and during 1890s the Oyster Commission had over seven thousand boats on its tax rolls. Using the 1873-1888 period as a base, the average annual yield of Maryland's natural oyster bars was about twelve million bushels. At forty-five cents per bushel, the Chesapeake oyster industry was a five-million-dollar industry. Throughout the 1880s the oyster-packing houses had been starved for workers to handle the mountain of oysters taken out of the Bay. In Cambridge at one point, Milford Phillips, a prominent oyster packer, employed over five hundred shuckers in his sheds on the Choptank. The state also benefited from the boom by taking seventy thousand dollars a year in license fees and fines, which offset the cost of maintaining an Oyster Navy.

In the winter of 1892-1893 the watermen of Chesapeake Bay began to reap the bitter harvest that Brooks had predicted. Oysters were scarce, and nine hundred dredgers scrambled on the Bay to catch the few that were left. At the end of that oyster season, the state of Maryland took its first faltering steps toward regulation of the industry. In the spring of 1893 the legislature passed a culling law that prohibited watermen from taking oysters less than two and one half inches from hinge to mouth. Also significantly, the state hired a dozen oyster inspectors to check oyster licenses and to make sure that the packing houses observed the new culling law. During this period the state was fortunate to have as oyster inspectors T. E. Wroten and W. E. Revelle. Both were conservation-minded watermen and helped to resolve numerous conflicts between watermen and the owners of packing houses. The packers, watermen charged, fixed prices for oysters up and down the Bay at forty-seven cents a bushel while they in turn charged astronomical prices to retailers. The watermen, the packers replied hotly, were "scrimping" oysters. By packing oysters lightly in a bushel tub, watermen gave what appeared to be a full load but actually was short of the legal requirement for a bushel. Further, packers complained of "bushwacking watermen" who acted as their own packers and attempted to steal customers from established companies.

It was also during this period that the Virginia oyster industry took a serious downturn owing to the rise of pests, disease, and municipal pollution in the Norfolk-Hampton Roads area. Thus the decline of the oyster harvest affected the entire region, intensified competition on the water, and accelerated conflicts between tongers and dredgers, watermen and packers, and watermen and police. By 1900 more packing houses on the Chesapeake closed annually than opened, and W. E. Revelle reported to Annapolis that a mean spirit prevailed among the people of the region. Tempers flared easily on the Potomac and on Pocomoke Sound, and few watermen ventured into either area unarmed.

According to Swepson Earle, who served for years as Maryland's conservation commissioner, the "toughest of the tough places on the Chesapeake in the 1890s was Rock Point on the Potomac River at the mouth of the Wicomico." In Earle's words, "Three killings a week created no civic resentment, while many weeks during the oyster season marked the departure from this life of as many as five or six men."

Black women canning oysters, *Harper's Weekly*, March 10, 1872.

Plainly put, Maryland and Virginia watermen despised one another; and as the Compact of 1785 allowed both states to catch oysters in the Potomac, the river became a battleground when dredgers left the exhausted beds of the Eastern Shore and attempted to take oysters from the rivermen of St. Mary's County and Westmoreland County, Virginia. "The great forebearance with which our Eastern Shore friends have been treated in the depredation of the oyster bars," complained the *St. Mary's Beacon*, "seems to have emboldened them to other breaches of the law." All along the Potomac communities complained of the "hideous behavior" of the dredgers and likened their arrival to that of the Vikings in Britain. When police attempted to arrest some dredgers at Millstone Landing in St. Mary's, these watermen went ashore, beat up several oyster police, and wrecked the local general store owned by C. M. Bohanan to show their contempt for the community.

During the winter of 1895, Father Charles K. Jenkins, the head of a Jesuit farm at Newtown Manor on St. Clement's Bay, was forced to call upon the state's attorney for St. Mary's County to protect church property from marauding Virginia dredge-boat crews. The winter was very hard, and hungry dredgers raided local farms for pigs, chickens, and sheep. When it seemed that there was to be no end to their depredations, area farmers and civic leaders formed a vigilante army and sprayed the dredge boats with bullets when the vessels were trapped in the ice at St. Clement's Bay. "Stay on the water, out of our churches, and out of our barns!" they warned.

While stories abounded of turmoil on the Potomac during this period, few illustrate the struggle to impose law and order on the river better than the experience of Douglas Russel in 1906. In that year Russel served as mate to Captain George W. Maddox on the Maryland Oyster Navy sloop *Bessie Jones* and was part of a police effort to keep dredgers off Cobb Bar in the river. That fall there had been several shoot-outs on the water and the police were anxious to restore order. One day in St. Mary's while Russel was at the old Bushwood Wharf, he quarreled with Alex Harris, an Oxford dredger, who vowed that the law could not keep him off Cobb Bar. "The law and my 45-70 rifle can do just that," Russel sternly replied. That night the *Bessie Jones* sighted Alex Harris's schooner on the bar. From a distance of seventy-five yards Russel began shooting at the halyards of the dredge boat, attempting to drop the sails for a capture. Harris returned the fire, and when the *Bessie Jones* closed near, Russel took a keen bead on Captain Harris and shot him. The large lead bullet from the 45-70 mushroomed when it hit his chest, and death was instantaneous. A few weeks later in Leonardtown, Russel was exonerated by a coroner's jury.

Yet when the dredge boats worked the Potomac they were a beautiful sight. In October 1911, Louis Sayer, a Baltimore writer, took a cruise on the buy boat *Ella F. Cripps* to the Potomac bound up for Breton Bay. "As we turned into the Bay at nine o'clock that night," he observed, "I thought we were approaching the lights of a city, but when we got deep into the bight, I found we were anchored among a fleet of five hundred vessels whose anchor lights I had taken for a settlement." While the rivermen hated the dredgers, added Sayer, none denied their consummate skill as sailors. On a gray afternoon when it began to cloud up and the wind started to blow harder, the dredges came up to the buy boat to unload their oysters. Little concerned with the howling wind and rolling waves in the mouth of the Potomac, the boats luffed easily under the stern of the *Cripps* "with jibs slapping and banging as they were hauled down and bows plunging, throwing the spray off in sheets."

Like the Potomac River, the Pocomoke Sound across the Bay was a much-fought-over treasure trove of oysters. In the Sound watermen pulled up oysters bigger than a man's hand and so rich in flavor that they commanded top prices in Baltimore. As oysters diminished elsewhere, conflict intensified in the Sound. Oystering on the Pocomoke Sound was more complicated than elsewhere on the Bay because it was the center of a boundary dispute between Maryland and Virginia that grew hotter with each passing year. By 1894 there was so much legal turmoil concerning the Pocomoke Sound that no one knew what the exact boundary between the two states was. The only thing that Maryland watermen knew for certain was that Pocomoke Sound contained about fifty-two square miles of oyster rocks that they were determined to fish and that Bobby Wharton, a Somerset waterman, was in jail at Onancock, Virginia.

During the winter of 1893-1894, Robert Wharton had been arrested for illegal oystering on Pocomoke Sound by the Virginia oyster militia and placed in jail by Sheriff John H. Wise of Accomac County, who was determined to prevent Marylanders from working the Sound. As Wharton refused to pay his five-hundred-dollar fine, he remained in jail while his friends appealed to Annapolis to secure his release. Marylanders like Wharton and his lawyers argued that the Pocomoke Sound was part of the Pocomoke River to which both states were guaranteed equal access by the Compact of 1785. Making it illegal for Maryland watermen to fish the Sound, argued Maryland's attorney general, violated the privileges and immunities clause of the Constitution. In response Virginia claimed that the Pocomoke Sound was a "separate and distinct body of water" not covered by the 1785 agreement, and the Supreme Court in *McCready* v. *Virginia* (1876) had previously held that her right to exclude Marylanders from the Sound was based not on citizenship but upon the "prerogative of her collective ownership of the oysters."

By the spring of 1894 both Virginia and Maryland reluctantly admitted that the ongoing dispute over access to the Pocomoke Sound between two soverign states would have to be solved by another round of litigation in the United States Supreme Court. The Court heard *Wharton* v. *Wise* on April 23, 1894, and supported Virginia's contention that the Pocomoke Sound was a distinct body of water and Marylanders had no right to take oysters in Virginia's part of the

Sound. The case was greeted by a storm of denunciation from Maryland politicians, who immediately launched a campaign to pay Wharton's fine and struggle against Virginia's "infamous" rule on the Sound.

Although the violence on the Sound was sharply diminished by 1900, animosities between Virginia and Maryland prevented the states from developing a comprehensive policy with regard to the fisheries of Chesapeake Bay. Thus did bad feelings and economic rivalry prevent Maryland from receiving much-needed seed oysters from the James River in Virginia. Similarly, Virginia was denied access to Maryland's oyster shell, so instrumental in revitalizing beds endangered by silt in the lower Chesapeake. In retrospect the Chesapeake Bay by the turn of the century was a good example of the "tragedy of the commons." Unlike private ownership of the means of production, a commons invites exploitation by all those who are competing for its benefits. Neither the watermen nor the states of Virginia and Maryland were willing to cooperate on a policy that would conserve the rapidly diminishing oyster resources of the Chesapeake. When oysters grew scarce in 1908, nearly two hundred dredge boats sailed around Cape Charles and headed up the Atlantic to Sinepuxent Bay and commenced to poach undersized oysters. The dredgers, pressed by declining fortunes in the Chesapeake, declared that law or no law, they intended to take oysters and would not be prevented from doing so. After being alerted by authorities in Worcester County, the Oyster Navy quickly rushed to the scene, but not before the watermen had severely damaged the Sinepuxent beds. The Sinepuxent was dotted with the sails of dredgers determined to get the last oyster; this mentality was in keeping with the times. As the watermen raped the beds, hunters in other parts of the country slaughtered the canvasback duck and buffalo to near-extinction.

Adversity is a stern and effective teacher, and in the years after 1900 the general decline of the oyster industry in Maryland prompted the state legislature to initiate new conservation measures on Chesapeake Bay. Concerned that new maritime technologies were outstripping the Bay's ability to replenish itself, the legislature prohibited steamers and powerboats from dredging oysters. The state also restricted oystering to bona fide residents of Maryland of one year who were "natural persons." This legal device protected individual oystermen from the competition of Baltimore seafood corporations. Licensing requirements were tightened and oystering in county waters was restricted to residents of that county. Joseph B. Seth, the commander of the state's Oyster Navy, divided the Chesapeake into several districts and stationed police sloops on patrol at the mouths of all of the rivers of the Eastern Shore and St. Mary's County. In the waters of Talbot, Kent, and Dorchester counties, where violence regularly flared, Seth stationed the *McLane* and the *Governor Thomas*, the most formidable boats in the oyster flotilla. In St. Mary's County waters two heavily armed schooners kept a watchful eye for oyster poachers in the Potomac. Seth also raised the salaries of his policemen and lengthened their annual tour of duty from six to twelve months.

In 1906 Maryland began its most ambitious attempt to identify the location and assess the condition of the oyster beds of the Chesapeake. This survey cost the state two hundred thousand dollars and was directed by Charles C. Yates, an engineer with the United States Coast and Geodetic Survey. From June 29, 1906, to August 17, 1912, Yates and his men triangulated, charted, buoyed, and sampled over one million acres of Chesapeake bottom. During the survey, Yates purchased a 135-foot steamboat, renamed her the *Oyster*, and made it home for himself and his thirty-man crew. After 159,530 soundings, Yates produced forty-two large-scale oyster charts; the *Yates Survey of the Oyster Bars of Maryland* is still in use today. The survey provided Maryland conservationists with one of the most scientifically precise studies ever made of the oyster reserves of the Chesapeake estuary.

HARD TIMES

During this period the leasing of oyster grounds was by far the most frustrating and controversial of Maryland's attempts to conserve Bay resources and regulate the oyster industry. Leasing oyster beds was an old idea in Maryland that was usually resurrected every twenty years by the legislature. As early as 1830 the state had granted one-acre oyster leases to Maryland citizens interested in growing oysters on the Bay's bottom. After the Civil War this law was amended to allow for five-acre leases. Oyster leasing, however, was disliked by watermen, who considered public fishing areas their own to use or ruin as they saw fit. In the county courts of Maryland oyster leasing was the source of so much legal acrimony that few Marylanders had the tenacity or the resources to fight the watermen. As one waterman put it, trying to get an oyster lease in Maryland was "about as easy as a fish escaping a gill net."

In 1906, B. Howard Haman, a legislator and energetic lawyer from Baltimore, took the initiative and introduced a new bill, subsequently known as the Haman Act, for oyster leasing and the cultivation of barren bottoms of the Bay. The bill, which easily passed the legislature, created the Board of Shell Fish Commissioners and directed it to lease barren bottoms of the Chesapeake for twenty years to Marylanders who would plant shell and seed oysters. The Haman Act also attempted to liberalize procedures for obtaining private oyster leases and called for a survey of submerged tidelands, primarily to determine the location of barren and productive bars. This endeavor resulted in the previously mentioned Yates Survey. During the first year that the Haman Act was in force, Eastern Shore watermen scrambled for oyster leases and squabbled in court over their rights. Soon, however, they grew tired of the leasing system and looked for ways to circumvent the act. Within a short time the watermen and their political allies in Annapolis were able to get fifty-four thousand acres of Chesapeake bottom previously classified as barren changed to productive natural bar. By 1914, the legislature also made it easy to challenge oyster leases in court. Thus did the conservationists' dream of a private oyster industry that would revitalize the Chesapeake founder because Annapolis lacked both the administrative vigor to administer the law and the political nerve to stand up to the watermen.

At times disputes over oyster leases were settled on the Bay at gunpoint. In September 1912, intense fighting broke out on the Connel oyster bar in the Manokin River when Ernest Cox, a Somerset dredger, attempted to raid a leased bar. Similarly, in January 1918, the *St. Mary's Beacon* reported that both Virginia and Maryland oyster navies were summoned to the Potomac to quell a leasing riot. The *Major Murrey* of Annapolis and the *Accomac* blasted out of the water several armed oyster boats that had attempted to plunder several leased bars in Port Tobacco Creek. Others chose to protect their bars, often without success, by erecting watchstands for armed guards directly over the beds. Many lease owners simply gave up rather than fight a western-style range war with their fellow watermen. Nothing sparked a feud among watermen quicker than the subject of oyster leasing. On October 2, 1936, a riot broke out in Princess Anne when a jury awarded an oyster planter the right to plant beds off Piney Island. According to the Baltimore *Sun*, "The fight was general all through the corridors of the court house and on the stairways after the court room was cleared. No arrests were made." According to Garret Power, an authority on Maryland oyster law, the courts and the watermen so effectively hamstrung the Haman Act that as late as 1952 only twelve thousand acres of bottom were under lease in Maryland waters of the Chesapeake.

Ironically, over the years the Oyster Commission and the Shell Fish Commission had more influence on oystermen in Connecticut and New York than in Maryland. After 1885 the practice of seeding leased oyster beds was widely observed in Long Island Sound. Seasonal regulations and the culling laws were also closely followed. At the time of the passage of the Haman Act, New York's watermen boasted that they already utilized "oyster farms" in the Long Island Sound to help regenerate their depressed industry.

In both prosperous and lean times the oyster industry did have one notable impact on the region. It prompted the construction of three types of sailing vessel, each with a distinct cycle of use on the Bay. The obscurely named pungy boat was a direct descendant of the Virginia pilot schooner and came into use in the oyster industry in the 1840s. Pungies were colorful boats painted in light pink and bottle green, with large keels and two tall raking masts. In the words of maritime historian Robert Burgess, "In all but superficial details of construction, the pungy was merely a reduced version of a Baltimore Clipper." The pungies were strong sailing vessels of twenty-three to sixty-nine tons and were long favored by oyster dredgers. While pungies like the *Amanda F. Lewis* were graceful and swift-sailing craft, they were heavy of draft and expensive. Gradually, as the dredgers began to work in the shallower areas of the Bay, they turned to the lighter draft and cheaper bugeyes to harvest oysters.

No sailboat dominated the lower Chesapeake in the 1880s like the bugeye. The bugeye was far cheaper to build and maintain and easier to handle than the pungy. Briefly described, the bugeye was a small, flat-bottomed centerboard schooner of three to fifteen tons, with a cabin aft. According to Eastern Shore folklore, the ship received its distinctive appellation because it maneuvered so well that it could "turn in a bug's eye." M. V. Brewington, an expert on Chesapeake Bay sailing craft, believes that the most plausible explanation is that the word derived from the scotch word *buckie*, meaning "oyster shell." As there were large numbers of Scottish immigrants in the Chesapeake area in the late nineteenth century, this explanation seems more likely than the argument that the boat was so named because it had distinctive hawseholes which when viewed from dead ahead were said to look like "bug's eyes." One of the best-known builders of this distinctive sailing craft was John Branford of Fairmount, Maryland; between 1883 and 1911 this resourceful shipwright constructed twenty-five bugeyes. Branford in the 1880s constructed a complete bugeye including sails and labor for $1,141.06. Of this he reaped $350 profit, which at 1,407 hours of labor averaged out to 25¢ an hour.

The 1890s witnessed the development of the skipjack, a new kind of sailing craft on the Chesapeake Bay. The skipjack, a product of changing economic conditions on the Bay, was a simple one-masted craft that was V-bottomed or deadrise, cheap to construct and easy to man. Named after the bluefish that at times "skip" across the surface of Chesapeake Bay, the skipjack was sufficiently easy to operate that it could be handled by one man in a pinch. By 1901 the skipjacks had replaced the pungy boats and the bugeyes as oyster dredges on the Bay because they could be more economically operated and maintained. Thus declining oyster resources sealed the fate of all complicated and expensive sailing craft used in the business. Of the skipjacks built after 1890, the largest was the *Robert L. Webster*, constructed by Sylvester Muir at Oriole. The boat was sixty feet on deck and was thirty-five gross tons in the water. Lacking the grace and the fine lines of the bugeye, the skipjack was an easily navigable and plodding work boat that enabled watermen to harvest oysters with a minimum of expense. Its appearance on the Bay was testimony to the hard times that were taking both the art and the romance out of oystering.

Whenever he looked out on Chesapeake Bay and saw the dredges, James B. Tawes remembered how he had once worked on one of those "backbreakers." There was no money in oystering, he instructed his sons, "only sweat, misery, and dumb pride." As proprietor of an oyster-packing company in Crisfield and founder in 1912 of Consumer's Ice Company, which chilled packed oysters, Tawes spoke from experience. During the boom of the seventies and eighties, Tawes had forsaken the Bay, plied a blacksmith's trade briefly, and then entered oyster packing and banking. Crisfield, Tawes wor-

100

ried, would not easily adapt to the changing times, and signs of strain were abundant. Many of the burlesque houses and saloons had closed, along with a score of packing houses; and Crisfield merchants followed the railroad several miles inland to become strawberry and peach brokers as truck crops assumed the ascendancy once held by seafood on the Eastern Shore. Also at this time the Bay had new enemies. In 1912 James B. Tawes had seen at first hand while he was a member of the State Fisheries Commission that the discharge of sewage from Washington, D.C., was having a harmful effect on the oyster beds of the Potomac. Later that year the Potomac River Oyster Pollution Commission reported to Governor Philip Goldsborough of Maryland and Governor William Hodges Mann of Virginia that the oysters were so contaminated above Blackstone Island that they could not be harvested.

Also in that lean year of 1912, hard-pressed oystermen from throughout the Eastern Shore descended upon Annapolis to complain that the state was trying to put them out of business. It was difficult to earn a livelihood, they argued, when the state limited the working season to fifty-eight days for dredging and one hundred days for tonging. Even with oysters ranging from sixty cents to a dollar a bushel, they claimed, the severe winters prevented tongers from making more than $300 a year, the minimum needed for economic survival. Dredgers, with more expensive equipment, earned only $1,836 and could scarcely afford to keep their boats in the water. Oystermen, especially those from Dorchester and Somerset, believed that the state Shell Fish Commission was nothing more than a tool of the large seafood packers who would gobble up the Bay with oyster leases once the watermen had been pushed into extinction. The oysters, they claimed, weren't really disappearing.

The oldtimers, recalled Viola Landon of Fairmount, said that the age of the almighty oyster came to an end in August 1914, when World War I erupted in Europe. While oysters at that time were more plentiful than in previous years, the season was a disaster because of the disruption of the trans-

Atlantic oyster trade with England. Also, the oyster boom in Louisiana and Florida made the domestic industry more competitive. Many dredge boat captains wound up heavily in debt, while others turned to commercial fishing and crabbing for seafood processors. The weather also seemed to conspire against the watermen. The winter of 1917-1918 was so severe that ice fourteen inches thick formed on the Choptank River. Ivy B. McNamara and his dredge boat crew made a sleigh and pulled their dredging equipment out on to the ice, and after chopping several holes through it, they pulled the dredges by hand across the beds. Off Tilghman Island the ice was so strong that trucks could be driven out to tongers who worked their oyster rakes through holes in the ice. During the "Big Freeze," as watermen called it, the ice began to stack up on the Bay and the roar of breaking ice could be heard for miles. Smith Islanders were isolated for seven weeks and were reduced to one small meal a day when the U.S. battleship *Ohio* entered the Bay and cut a ship channel. Yet despite the hardships of life on the Bay, surprisingly few left the water, and the Chesapeake seemed to cling to its old maritime ways longer than other bodies of water. The fact that they were becoming anachronisms in an urban age of skyscrapers and steel didn't seem to bother the watermen.

Throughout the war and the "roaring twenties," there was little money in the maritime communities of the Eastern Shore. Most people lived by barter and trade, exchanging salt fish for flour and meal and then making underwear and clothes out of the bags the flour and meal had come in. Everyone had hogs; when oysters and crabs were slack, many watermen served as guides for the increasing number of prosperous businessmen who came down from Philadelphia and New York to hunt ducks. Others risked arrest in a new form of warfare with the Maryland naval militia.

Following the enactment of Prohibition, the Maryland Oyster Navy was assigned to patrol the Bay and apprehend "rum runners" who were smuggling liquor up the Chesapeake and into the state. Watermen on the Potomac River and on the waters of Charles and St. Mary's counties were deeply involved in the illicit whiskey trade and helped unload bootleggers' boats at night for shipment by truck to Washington. For his efforts each man received a half gallon of whiskey, which could easily be turned into cash. On many occasions watermen found themselves on small powerboats run by Baltimore gangsters trading rifle fire with the oyster police as they hurried to safety in the waters of Virginia. Sometimes, when capture appeared inevitable, they simply dumped the cargo overboard. In November 1928, at the start of the oyster season, Captain Will Smith of Tylerton, Smith Island, caught thirty-six gallon jugs of "white mule" in his oyster dredge, which proved to be more valuable than oysters to the thirsty citizens of Crisfield.

Long accustomed to hard work and lean times, the watermen were little affected at first by the depression of the 1930s. Oysters, remembers Alex Kellam of Crisfield, had few buyers even at the low price of thirty cents a bushel. After seven weeks of oystering on a skipjack, Kellam recalls, he had less than thirty dollars to show for his hard work. Rather than the nostrums of the New Deal and President Roosevelt, it was the weather, especially the terrible hurricane of 1933, that transformed the lives of the oystermen of Chesapeake Bay.

On August 19, 1933, a furious rainstorm lashed the Eastern Shore. After four days of pelting rains, the sky turned black and a hurricane came howling across Chesapeake Bay. In Crisfield the tide rose sharply and local merchants scrambled to save their goods from the encroaching salt water. By 5:00 P.M. on August 23, the tide had risen seven feet. On Smith Island the tide rose so fast that it caught whole families in the midst of their summer canning. By 3:00 P.M. the Chesapeake began to flood the village of Tylerton. Nola Tyler's father looked at the ominous sky and ordered his family to eat supper quickly. "Don't take time to wash the supper dishes," he warned, "because the tide is at the fourth doorstep!" As the rising sea engulfed the small village, residents hurried to the small church, which was located on the highest ground on the island. Many people had to evacuate their homes by boat. In Nola Tyler's words, "The tide was coming in the windows and was up past our waists. Grandpa was the last one to get on the boat. It was all Pappa and Thomas could do to push the boat against the strong waves. Finally about 4:30 P.M. we got to the church where other families had gone for safety and shelter." Within a short time the tide had reached the church and the foundation began to snap and crack. Everyone was frightened; there was no other place to go. Suddenly at 9:00 that night the wind shifted and the waters began to recede. Some were praying and thanking God, some were so tired that they were asleep on the pews of the choir and on benches. The next morning it was a struggle to return home. Boats had drifted on to the roads, trees had fallen everywhere, and the air reeked of dead livestock.

Throughout the Chesapeake there had been heavy flooding: farms were destroyed, commerce and communication disrupted. The rivers of the region turned yellow and malevolent and spilled millions of gallons of fresh water into the Bay, destroying thousands of acres of oyster beds. That winter, for the first time in their lives, many watermen reluctantly accepted help from state relief agencies. After the hurricane of 1933, oystering never sprang back on Tangier Sound, and even those oysters that watermen did catch sold at far less than thirty cents a bushel. Given the desperate circumstances that prevailed as the Depression lengthened, watermen attempted to pirate oysters in the Potomac once again, and on November 20, 1937, the Maryland oyster police powerboat *Kent* sailed into the river to restore order. This time the police were armed with machine guns, and after several bursts of fire the dredgers retreated. Following the outbreak of World War II in 1941, many oystermen like Alex Kellam finally quit the water and went to work in the Bethlehem Fairfield Shipyards of Baltimore for an unprecedented wage of 72½¢ an hour. Others joined the navy and coast guard and helped to pilot ships in the Bay and along the south Atlantic coast. Given the overwhelming manpower needs of the war effort, there were few able-bodied men left on the Chesapeake to catch oysters, and the beds remained fallow for several years. Not until the 1950s would large numbers of men return to the Bay to follow the water; and during the "mini oyster boom" of these years the clatter of machine guns and the popping of rifles would once again be heard on the Chesapeake.

NUMSEN'S BLOCK.

WM. NUMSEN & SONS,

PRESERVERS, PICKLERS,

OYSTER PACKERS, &c.

Office, 18 Light Street,

Factories at Jackson St., Federal Hill, and German St., near Green St.

Chapter 6

GUNFIRE ON THE POTOMAC

C OLONIAL BEACH, VIRGINIA, was an unlikely setting for
the final chapter of the Chesapeake oyster wars. Until
the Depression the town was primarily a popular
resort on the Potomac that catered more to tourists than to
watermen. On Sundays from May to September steamboats
from Washington cruised down the Potomac and discharged
hundreds of passengers who came down on vacation to bask
in the sun, bathe in the river, and ride the Ferris wheel.
Unfortunately, the hard times of the 1930s and the end of the
Bay steamers dealt a heavy blow to river resorts like Colonial
Beach on both sides of the Chesapeake. Accessible only by a
narrow highway that snaked through the rolling hills of
Westmoreland County, Colonial Beach after World War II
was shunned by affluent middle-class motorists who sped to
Virginia Beach and Ocean City on weekends. By the 1950s
Colonial Beach was a resort in decline, trying hard to stave
off decay and ruin. The proprietors of the old hotels and faded
stores tried to revive business by introducing slot machines
and successfully attracted a hard-drinking, hard-gambling
blue-collar crowd from Washington and Richmond. The
weekend gamblers loved the "slots" and some store owners
bragged that the machines brought in an extra two hundred
dollars a month. Though tawdry, Colonial Beach became a
poor man's Las Vegas.

In addition to the slot machines, Colonial Beach featured
another kind of gambling whose stakes were far higher than
any storefront game of chance. Dredging oysters on the Potomac was not for the faint-hearted gambler. Maryland Marine

Police, armed with machine guns and rifles, awaited the Virginia waterman willing to risk his life for a fast three hundred dollars by illegally dredging oysters on the river.

In 1942, after decades of low prices and poor harvests, watermen from Virginia and Maryland discovered "a damn big oyster strike" on the Potomac's Swann Point bar. The oysters were large, white, and flavorful, and brought high prices. Inasmuch as most watermen had either been drafted into the war effort or had joined the coast guard, those who remained earned good money pirating oysters with a dredge. When it came to choosing between eight hours of hard labor pulling up oysters with legal shaft tongs or one hour's work dredging, watermen invariably chose the latter. During World War II it was difficult for Maryland to enforce the oyster laws because most of her boats had been lent to the coast guard. Across the Potomac in Virginia, the Dahlgren Artillery Range used the river for target practice; when the red flag was raised up on the bluff, all boats were forbidden in that section of the river in front of the installation. Thus watermen often eluded the oyster police by threading a dangerous course through the heavy whoosh and spray of artillery shells impacting on the water. "We used to give them artillery officers up at Dahlgren the fits," recalls a retired waterman. "But it sure was an easy way to get away from them Maryland police boats."

After the war illegal dredging of Potomac oysters began in earnest. With the removal of price controls, oysters, which had brought only fifteen cents a bushel in Colonial Beach during the depths of the Depression, commanded two dollars. One of the happiest residents of Colonial Beach at this time was Landon Curley, the town's shrewd and affable oyster packer. By 1947 a mini oyster boom on the Potomac and Chesapeake was in full swing and over 150 work boats tied up on Curley's wharf on Monroe Creek. During the oyster season Land Curley could always be found hurrying around his packing house and docks with a bouncing gait. Curley during this time was buying all the oysters he could get and his "Pearl of Perfection" oysters were popular in the mid-Atlantic region. Those willing to risk dredging oysters were befriended by Curley, who lent them boats to obtain their booty.

During this time conflicts with the Maryland oyster police differed from the battles of the late nineteenth century. In the 1940s and 1950s oyster piracy was conducted on a smaller scale and involved fewer watermen. Passions, however, continued to run high, and bullets whistled on the Potomac within a two-hour drive of the nation's capital as the marine police of the Tidewater Fisheries Commission sought to end poaching and impose Maryland's authority on the river. The battleground was a stretch of river twenty-five miles long extending downstream from the Potomac Bridge where busy Route 301 crossed.

After the war over 170 watermen from both sides of the Potomac were poaching oysters. Most of these watermen used high-powered motorboats that enabled them to dredge with great speed and efficiency. These boats entered the river from St. Mary's County and Colonial Beach at night and ran without lights. Most of these boats were from eighteen to forty feet in length with a light draft and had a powerful Mercury or Johnson motor in the stern that enabled them to run circles around the oyster police. As many of these boats fled from the police into shallow water to escape apprehension, they became known as the Mosquito Fleet, a term used to describe many of the small boats used in the swamps and harbors of the South Pacific during World War II. Most of the fleet's watermen were young men who believed that stealing oysters was like stealing watermelons. It was nothing to get serious about.

Annapolis, however, viewed the matter differently. Besides oyster poaching, there was the larger issue of Maryland's sovereignty and her control of the Potomac River. Unless the dredgers were vanquished, Maryland feared that Virginia would seize upon this opportunity to expand her authority on the Potomac River—an issue the two states had feuded over since colonial times. Maryland also harbored a grudge against Virginia that stemmed from the fact that since the seventeenth century Maryland had lost every territorial dispute that it had with Virginia. As the start of the 1947-1948 oyster season drew near, the Maryland legislature ordered a thorough housecleaning of its Tidewater Fisheries Police. The oyster police, complained many legislators, had become a retirement home for aged officers who took bribes from packers and watermen. Many of these were retired, and others transferred to desk jobs. New recruits were added, and by September the police flotilla numbered ninety-seven men and forty vessels. Captain Chester Cullison, a highly esteemed veteran oyster police officer, was transferred to the Potomac River and made commander of a four-boat force. Cullison's orders were brief: end all illegal dredging on the river.

Cullison's motorboat, the *Pocomoke*, was outfitted with a war-surplus water-cooled machine gun, and he warned watermen from St. Mary's and Colonial Beach that there would be a new order on the Potomac. Within a week, Cullison arrested four dredgers and confiscated seven boats, including the *Venus*, a powerboat owned by Landon Curley. Much to the consternation of Curley and his friends at Colonial Beach, Cullison took the confiscated *Venus* and recommissioned her as a Maryland police patrol boat.

A few watermen at first refused to take Cullison seriously. "There was one fellow that used to aggravate me near about to death," recalled Cullison. "One day we chased him into water too shallow for us to follow and he yelled 'Why don't you shoot?' We pulled the *Pocomoke* around and went in to lead him. Machine gunned him right along the water line. He moved her and she sank." Not many watermen, Cullison declared, would be building fancy homes in Colonial Beach on three-hundred-dollar-a-night profits from dredged oysters. Throughout that winter there were many high-speed chases on the Potomac reminiscent of western movies where an armed posse chased bank robbers. Often a

Potomac River oyster police, *Pocomoke* and others. Courtesy: The Baltimore *Sun*.

slow dredger in danger of being intercepted by a Maryland patrol boat would be abandoned with its throttle wide open while the crew men jumped to a faster boat and made their getaway.

When Cullison learned that January that Virginians were dredging off Cedar Point, he went after the boats. As they were about to outrun him, he let fly with a few machine-gun bursts. Two boats sank and the rest scattered for home. Later Cullison sailed the *Pocomoke* up to Swann Point and repeated the process with the same results. Afterwards Cullison discovered that in two encounters he had used up the small supply of ammunition that was supposed to last the entire season.

Virginia and Maryland watermen howled with indignation over the "machine-gun happy Captain" and Cullison was summoned back to Annapolis to face a panel of inquiry headed by Edward Warfield, chairman of the Maryland Conservation Commission. When Warfield demanded to know what the shooting was all about, Cullison summarized his long career as a law enforcement officer on the Bay and extolled the Maryland oyster industry. He talked about his frustrations with the Mosquito Fleet that was pirating oysters from Maryland waters and the threat its actions posed to conserving natural resources on the Potomac. After he had finished, the commissioner eyed him coldly. Finally after a long silence Warfield spoke. "Captain Cullison," he said sternly, "do you need any more bullets?"

Cullison returned to the Potomac with renewed determination. He usually could be found at the wheel of his boat during oyster season; the usual tools of his profession were close at hand—a brass oyster measure to see if oysters were of legal size, a pair of battered binoculars, and a coffee-stained copy of the oyster laws of Maryland. Outside on the bow of the boat the machine gun was loaded and a rifle was near by. Occasionally Cullison used his screeching radio to keep in touch with the other boats as well as the Tidewater Fisheries Commission headquarters in Annapolis.

THE OYSTER WARS

In most cases success for the oyster police on the Potomac didn't mean an arrest. Police officers were happy when they got close enough to a dredger so that he was forced to abandon his equipment and throw his dredge overboard. Some watermen marked their dredges with buoys when they tossed them away. The police, however, pulled them up and used them as evidence. More resourceful pirates wrapped their buoys in bags of salt. The buoy would sink at first and elude the police. Later, as the salt melted, the buoy popped to the surface and a waterman could retrieve his lost dredge. The financial costs of "chasing drudgers" were enormous, and all in all, said Captain Cullison, patrolling the Potomac was "aggravating business." Cullison and his men spoke of a "nine-dredge night" or a "fourteen-dredge night" with the same satisfaction that a hunter uses to describe a good day of duck shooting. The one most frustrating fact for the oyster police was that Virginia watermen were protected by the Potomac Compact of 1785, which stated that Virginia watermen had to be tried in their own courts regardless of the state which made the arrest on the river. Much to the annoyance of Maryland officials, Virginia's courts were extraordinarily lenient towards their watermen: most poachers got off with a reprimand and a small fine.

While the Virginia marine police gave assistance to Cullison and his river flotilla, relations between the two marine police forces on the Potomac cooled considerably after the machine-gun incidents. Virginia's police reflected Richmond's annoyance at Maryland's strong-arm tactics on the river whose fisheries they shared. Not to be intimidated, Richmond dispatched a seaplane to patrol its side of the Chesapeake Bay and to arrest poachers found in Virginia waters.

In June 1949, David Acree, a Virginia Fisheries deputy, riding in a seaplane above Chesapeake Bay, spotted a Maryland workboat crabbing two miles inside the Virginia boundary. He promptly landed beside the craft and ordered Earl

Nelson, a sixty-year old waterman from Crisfield, to steer toward a Virginia patrol boat. After a sharp exchange of words, Nelson refused to move and Acree attempted to grab the tiller. The two men started to fight and during the struggle Acree's rifle went off, dropping Nelson to the deck. Acree panicked, boarded his plane, and flew back to base while two fellow crabbers rushed to Nelson's aid. When they finally got to his boat, the rescuers found Nelson bleeding from a severed femoral artery. Before they could get him ashore to a hospital in Crisfield he was dead. Although Virginia authorities conducted a hearing later, no disciplinary action was taken against Acree.

Such incidents only tended to worsen relations that were bad to begin with between the two states. Casting a sharp eye on the controversy, the Baltimore *Sun* blamed the oyster police of both states for "stirring up the so-called oyster war." Matters had reached a point, declared the *Sun*, where people were "hard pressed to tell whether the conflict was a gang war or a neighborhood game of cops and robbers."

On the Maryland side of the Potomac, one thing was perfectly clear—the Tidewater Fisheries police were trigger-happy. Back in those days, remembers Captain Ellsworth Hoffman of the state marine police, the Tidewater Fisheries Commission encouraged men to use their firearms. "They considered it a big thing and you were looked up to if you shot at dredgers," said Hoffman. Also, the men on the Maryland force were poorly trained. Oyster policemen were appointed by local politicians in the legislature and "if they liked your looks, they gave you a badge, a gun, and an arrest book." Police training in those days consisted of a week's stint at an old navy base near Solomon's Island that was remembered more for its beer parties than instruction. While David Wallace, the Maryland Tidewater Fisheries Commissioner, subsequently removed the machine guns from the boats, this was largely a public relations gesture. The oyster police still remained quick on the draw.

THE OYSTER WARS

A short time later Virginia announced that its legislature would allow powerboat dredging in certain areas of the Potomac and indicated that it would give refuge to violators of the Maryland law, which prohibited any kind of dredging on the river. Once again the states thrashed in the snare of the Compact of 1785, which stated that whatever one state legislated with respect to the river, the other had to concur with or the legislation was null and void. Virginia's dredging initiative was sent to Annapolis, where Maryland legislators hooted it down in a chorus of obscenities. Thus by 1950, as one observer of the Potomac wrote, "the mere presence of a dredge on a powerboat in Maryland waters was enough to send conservation police up in blue smoke and to entitle the boat operator to confiscation of vessel, up to one thousand dollars fine, and from one to three years imprisonment."

While the two states feuded, Maryland oyster policemen were preoccupied with a scandal that threatened to destroy the authority of the marine force. In 1951 Amos Creighton, chief inspector for the Tidewater Fisheries Commission, sent a seaplane to meet a police boat and bring back several bushels of oysters to be served at an Annapolis political banquet. The pilot located the boat and pitched alongside. Much to his amazement the pilot, who was also a police officer, found the boat dredging illegally, and four oyster police officers were doing the work. The pilot confiscated the dredge and raised a furor in departmental headquarters in Annapolis. Creighton narrowly missed being fired, and the episode, which was gleefully reported in the newspapers, cast doubt on the commitment of the oyster police to uphold the maritime laws of Maryland. If the oyster police broke the rules, argued watermen, they would too.

The Creighton affair occurred just as Police Inspector Robert Lee Shores was given the unhappy task of enforcing the Maryland law on the Potomac. The only way that he could spare his men from ridicule was to project an image of toughness. He distributed 30-30 rifles to his men with ample supplies of ammunition. Scandal or no scandal, Shores

114

vowed, the oyster police were going to guard the Potomac. For several winters thereafter the waters of the Potomac were enlivened by Mosquito Fleeters who in their powerboats whooped with derision at the pursuing pistol-firing oyster police, who clung none too securely to their light outboard boats. Meanwhile, Virginians sat on the shore and watched the farce through their binoculars. The oyster pirates clearly had the upper hand; they had faster boats, a highly integrated system of spies and lookouts, and the friendly shelter of a thousand creeks and coves. Also, to add insult to injury, reported Captain Chester Cullison, some of the worst offenders came from Maryland.

Finally, to prevent further disintegration of Maryland's authority on the Bay and the Potomac, Governor Theodore McKeldin appointed John Tawes chairman of Maryland's Tidewater Fisheries Commission. A protégé of Senator Harry Phoebus of Somerset County and a tough-minded administrator, Tawes replaced Arthur Brice, who passed into political oblivion after being charged with shooting ducks in a baited blind. The commission had a reputation of being a revolving door for political hacks, and McKeldin urged Tawes to shake up the bureaucracy and the marine force; the new commissioner began his job with a sense of dedication that bordered on the fanatic. Tawes liked to hire tough young men right out of the army who were willing to fight if challenged for his oyster police force. The new commissioner was ubiquitous on the Bay and used radio telephones to stay in almost constant touch with his marine police. Tawes was determined to end illegal dredging on the Potomac, and, the commissioner snorted, he was going to protect the natural resources of Maryland even if it meant patrolling the Potomac around the clock. "They're working us to death," complained Captain Cullison, "but there are fewer dredgers now than at the beginning of the season." Many a dredger's expensive outboard engine was destroyed by Captain Joseph Davis, commander of the *Venus*, who had the fastest boat in the Oyster Navy and the best marksmen. They were under orders, Captain Davis said, to knock out the dredgers' engines and not hit the men. Yet on a cold winter night when visibility was next to nothing, he added, it was "damned spooky out on that river." Sometimes a nervous oyster policeman would fire his weapon before he was sure what he was shooting at.

Watermen liked black moonless nights best for oyster poaching, especially when there was a light drizzle of rain and the fog hugged the water's surface. A powerboat would cruise slowly with the dredge dragging the bottom. Experienced watermen could tell by the feel of the line when the dredge touched oysters. Once they found a bar, the skipper threw a marker overboard—an inner tube supporting an upside-down bushel basket. Inside the basket was a lantern with the wick turned down until the barest flicker of light showed through the basket. Thus the helmsman could keep the light in sight as the boat circled it slowly while the crew worked the dredge. At dawn, with its motors muffled, the boat crept through the fog toward Monroe Creek and the Virginia shore. If he sighted the police, the captain opened the engine to full throttle and made a mad dash for Monroe Harbor. Awaiting on the dock in the early dawn was Landon Curley, hands on hips, barking orders to a pack-house crew.

In the fall of 1955, Commissioner Tawes, with the help of an attorney general's ruling, decided that all Virginia oystermen working the Potomac should be charged a Maryland export tax. He took this action in spite of the Compact provision that Virginia watermen should have equal rights on the Potomac. For Richmond, Tawes's act was the last straw. Prior to Tawes's coming, Captain William Ryland of the Virginia Marine Police and Captain Chester Cullison had cooperated on law enforcement matters on the river. Now such efforts became impossible. Said Captain Ryland: "We pulled our boats out when Tawes put that tax on. A man from the Maryland side of the Potomac River doesn't pay this tax and we don't think that it is fair to the Virginia Potomac waterman." For two months Tawes wavered and then withdrew the export tax. Suddenly in January 1956 he reimposed it with a vengeance after acquiring a fast surplus military seaplane. Many oystermen from Colonial Beach refused to pay the tax and, rather than "tong oysters for Mr. Tawes," they switched to illegal nighttime dredging. As police patrols harassed the watermen, dredgers like Bozo Atwell grew more defiant.

To Wilson "Bozo" Atwell provoking the Maryland oyster police into a chase on the river was even more fun than dredging oysters. A tall, rangy twenty-nine-year-old waterman from Colonial Beach, Atwell despised John Tawes and the Maryland Tidewater Fisheries Commission and was not afraid to fight. Once when the Maryland oyster police tried to capture him, Atwell ran his boat up a creek and right into the marsh grass. Running like a swamp deer, Bozo dashed to his nearby truck and pulled out his hunting rifle, taking a steady aim at the police officers. After several anxious moments, the police backed off. They knew that Bozo Atwell was "just damned crazy enough to start shooting" if they tried to seize his boat. When Landon Curley offered him the chance to serve as captain of the *Little Craig*, Atwell eagerly accepted. The *Craig* was a fifty-foot former German navy powerboat that Curley had picked up on the military surplus market. He also had installed a big six-cylinder Hall Scott motor in the stern, and the craft could "go like Hell" on the Potomac when the police attempted to close in.

On the night of October 26, 1956, the weather on the river was exceptionally severe; the wind was blowing hard and cold and visibility was almost nil. Atwell and three other men were heavily dressed in oilskins and worked an oyster bar quietly. All that could be heard in the darkness was the constant slapping of the waves against the *Little Craig*. Bozo's boat, however, was not the only craft out on the river that night. Captain Thomas Noble's oyster-patrol boat was a short distance away, idling along through the spray and darkness.

Noble listened continuously to the windward, trying to hear engine sounds above the beating of the waves against the hull. Suddenly Noble heard a deep-throated rumble in the distance and worked his boat toward the sound. Before he saw anything else, Noble spied the light marker floating on an inner tube. The mist was so heavy that the two boats almost rubbed gunwales before they saw each other. When Atwell's boat crossed the working light, Noble turned on his spotlight. Four surprised dredgers were caught in the glare and Bozo raced to the stern to gun the engine. The *Little Craig* jumped ten feet and suddenly stalled, her massive engine choked with gasoline. The police boat crashed into the *Craig*'s port bow and Noble's mate ran forward with a line to lash the two boats together. Outraged by the turn of events, Bozo grabbed a hatchet and ran forward toward the mate. Atwell later said that he was only attempting to cut the line, but the mate insisted that had Bozo caught him, he would have cleaved his skull. Noble picked up his rifle and ordered the oystermen away from the engine. Atwell ignored him and after a few coughs the Hall Scott engine roared and the *Craig* surged ahead. Both Noble and the mate blazed away at the escaping boat. Suddenly Noble felt a numbing blow in his right arm and dropped his rifle, wounded from a wild shot from his mate's revolver. The *Little Craig* sped off, leaving the patrol boat and its wounded skipper behind. Later, on shore, Bozo Atwell laughed at "those fellows plugging away at us like we were kidnappers or something and all they do is shoot each other."

The next day the Tidewater Fisheries Commission charged Bozo Atwell with assault with attempt to kill. Virginia troopers put Bozo under five hundred dollars bail as "a fugitive from Maryland," but Governor Thomas Stanley refused to allow his extradition. Annapolis raged at Virginia for six months before a Westmoreland County judge found Atwell guilty of poaching oysters. The judge also ordered Bozo to produce the boat for confiscation, a matter that caused a flurry of activity in Colonial Beach because Landon Curley had sold the *Craig* to a Washington yacht broker. Curley bought back the boat and surrendered it to the Tidewater

Fisheries Commission. Neither Bozo Atwell nor Landon Curley, however, was discouraged. They knew that law enforcement was a sorry affair on the Potomac River, and Virginia's withdrawal of her officers had been interpreted by Virginia's watermen to mean "Go to it boys! We're looking the other way." While Governor McKeldin fumed in Annapolis over the recent turn of events on the Potomac, Captain Thomas Noble became the innocent victim of the Bozo Atwell fiasco. To placate the governor, the Tidewater Fisheries Commission ordered Noble into early retirement and ended his short and promising career as a marine police officer.

Three months after Noble was shot Captain Chester Cullison, now commanding the *Tiny Lou*, ran across Harvey King and his crew dredging oysters early one morning off Colonial Beach. Harvey King was a beer-drinking fun-loving daredevil, and when Landon Curley offered him the helm of his boat, the *Miss Ann*, King smiled and declared that he would give the Maryland police a merry chase. One night in January 1957, when Harvey King saw the *Chesapeake* and the *Tiny Lou* plunging across the river toward him, he yelled to his crew men Albert Rollins and Dempsey Roy, "Drop the damn dredge and let her rip!" The engine of the *Miss Ann* thundered into action and the boat surged across the water toward Colonial Beach with Cullison and his men in hot pursuit. As the morning light cleared the mists, spectators on shore saw one of the most spectacular chase scenes in the history of the Potomac River conflict. The boats were crashing up and down on the waves and the Virginians could see that the *Miss Ann* was making a wild dash for the safe waters of Monroe Creek, which curved around the residential area of Colonial Beach. Pursued now by two police boats and a seaplane, Harvey King's fun had just begun. The Maryland officers poured a rain of bullets from rifles and pistols while King maneuvered the *Miss Ann* in an evasion pattern that would have sparked the envy of men experienced in naval combat in

119

the South Pacific. As King raced toward Monroe Creek, bullets tore two holes in the side of his boat. Yet during his hour-long baptism by fire, Harvey King went unscathed. Bullets skipped across the water, several slamming into the walls of the Walcot Tavern on the beach. While the chase went on a crowd of some four hundred persons lined the Virginia shore to cheer the pursued and curse the police. When the shooting grew heavy, many crouched behind cars as bullets socked into the river bank and ripped through trees. Miraculously, no one on shore was hurt.

A Virginia state trooper awaited Harvey King on shore and later charged him with the relatively minor offense of concealing the name and number of his boat. Maryland, on the other hand, had had several encounters with Harvey King and his crew and now demanded his extradition on charges of unlawful oyster dredging, nonpayment of the oyster export tax, and resisting arrest. King was the model of composure as the Virginia and Maryland authorities quarreled over him. To curious onlookers on Monroe Creek, King displayed six pistol holes, six rifle holes, and two shotgun patterns in the *Miss Ann*. Only their heavy oilskin foul-weather gear, King claimed, had protected him and his crew from the spray of the shotgun pellets. Local officials did not, however, share King's composure. Mayor Costenbader of Colonial Beach declared that in the use of such deadly fire Maryland had shown "a complete lack of judgment." Costenbader also feared that indiscriminate gunfire on the Potomac would hurt the town's tourist industry. In Richmond Governor Stanley called a press conference to protest the shootings, claiming that the oyster police had needlessly imperiled the lives of the Colonial Beach citizenry and demanding assurances that there would be no recurrence of such behavior.

Such assurances were not forthcoming from Annapolis. In a bravado-filled letter to Governor Stanley, McKeldin defended his police and warned the Virginia governor that "when lawbreakers use high speed boats, we must use firearms." Within a week after the King incident McKeldin obtained an extra one hundred thousand dollars from the legislature to purchase new high-powered patrol boats.

King, meanwhile fought extradition. "A Virginia waterman," he claimed. "ain't got a snow ball's chance in Hell in a Maryland court. If they want us, they're gonna have to come and get us. The boat too!" Maryland wanted them all right, and Police Inspector Robert Lee Shores swore out the extradition warrant; after some public posturing, Governor Stanley reluctantly agreed to allow the watermen to stand trial in Maryland. In court King and his crew told the jury that they were not dredging, merely "sounding for an oyster lump" to be tonged later that day. To the watermen's astonishment, they were acquitted. When Harvey King returned to Colonial Beach many older watermen advised him to stop showing off. A grown man, they said, had better things to do than to play hide-and-seek with the oyster police. Besides, recalls Calvin Dickinson, a retired waterman, "There were so many police on the river that you couldn't make any money drudging oysters." Unless the boys from Colonial Beach stopped making the oyster police "so damned crazy," warned the mayor, somebody was liable to get badly hurt.

A few weeks later a Virginia dredger was rammed so hard by a Maryland police boat that his stern fell off. The speed of the boat was enough to keep the water out until the dredger slowed down to beach her. The boat sank immediately. The Maryland oyster police reported coyly that the stern had merely "fallen off during a high-speed pursuit." Also at this time Governor McKeldin sent a fast, specially equipped PT boat into the Potomac to work in concert with the patrol boat *Honga River*. McKeldin also announced that Maryland was abrogating the Compact of 1785 and would take full control of the river. Henceforth, he declared, an oysterman on the Potomac would be subject to the laws and governance of Maryland, and oyster pirates would be tried exclusively in Maryland courts. The final version of the abrogation bill passed the Maryland legislature in the spring of 1957. Shortly afterwards the Tidewater Fisheries Commission announced that it was in full control of the river and now expected "a quiet time on the Potomac."

In one respect the commission was right, for the locus of the noisy conflict between the two states shifted from the Potomac to the velvet-draped courtroom of the United States Supreme Court. Virginia's attorney general scurried to Washington to protest that Maryland had no right to end the Potomac Compact without Virginia's approval. Maryland in turn complained to the Supreme Court justices that Virginia historically had acted in bad faith by not prosecuting oyster violators as vigorously as the Tidewater Fisheries Commission would have liked to have done and should therefore suffer the loss of equal fishing rights on the river. At times the attorneys from both states became highly charged, and the court, unwilling to make a prompt decision on the matter, referred the case to Stanley F. Reed, a retired Supreme Court justice. After examining the Compact of 1785 and listening to the arguments of both states, Reed concluded that the only remedy to a legal conflict that might last decades was an out-of-court settlement; he urged the formation of a bistate commission that would regulate affairs on the Potomac. Faced with the alternatives of protracted legal strife or a settlement, both states grumbled their consent and in the summer of 1958 drew up a preliminary charter and legal code for governance of the river.

While the solons in the legislature and the Supreme Court came to grips with the thorny legal issue of the Potomac fisheries, life continued as usual in Colonial Beach. As the 1958-1959 season advanced, oystermen were earning $3.25 a bushel for oysters; there seemed to be plenty on the bars, and a dredger had to be crazy, said many local watermen, to think that he could outrun the PT boat of the Maryland oyster police. Watermen congregated in Landon Curley's pool hall and luncheonette adjacent to the packing house on Monroe Creek, and there were always men around to wager a Dr. Pepper or a fiver on a game of eight ball. In the evening oystermen liked to listen to Berkeley Muse tell jokes about the tourists who came to gamble at Colonial Beach. "They're just dying to give us their money," Muse laughed as he cued a smashing drive into the freshly racked balls.

Practically everyone in Colonial Beach liked Berkeley Muse. Good-natured and respected by community leaders, Muse speculated in real estate, farmed, and occasionally tonged oysters. Both he and his father owned some waterfront property which they were busily converting to lots for sale to out-of-town people wanting to build summer cottages. Berkeley Beach, Muse boasted, would soon become a thriving vacation community. Although a shrewd businessman, Berkeley Muse had a weakness for his friends from his old hell-raising days before he had gotten married and fathered three children. On the night of April 7, 1959, Muse was racking up the pool table for a game of nine ball when his old friend Harvey King sauntered in and merrily announced that later that evening he was going to dredge oysters. "I don't give a damn about the police," he laughed. When Harvey King was up to mischief it was hard to resist him, and he said he needed a third man to help him and John Griffith man the dredge. He had a fast boat that would run circles around the police, King bragged, and they'd just dredge a few bushels for fun. Berkeley Muse left the pool hall around 9:00 P.M., went home and got a few hours' sleep, and started out with King and Griffith around three o'clock in the morning.

Unfortuntely for the dredgers, Howard Shenton, chief inspector of the Tidewater Fisheries Commission, had arranged a stakeout on the river that week following several reports of illegal dredging. He sent the PT boat, now christened the *McKeldin*, upstream and ordered the *Honga River* near the mouth of Monroe Bay. Shenton remained on shore, maintaining radio contact with the two boats.

The mist rising off the dark water of the Potomac in the eerie April dawn seemed like smoke rising from some troubled netherworld and screened King and his men from detection. By 4:30 A.M., when they had harvested about seven bushels of oysters, the mist began to clear. Suddenly the dredgers spied the *Honga River* lunging toward them out of a fogbank. King let out the throttle and raced toward Monroe Bay. About four hundred feet from the beach at Reno Pier Inspector Shenton spotted the dredgers and told his police over his radio to open fire. Police Officers Harvey Cooke and Barnes Braun fired a half dozen warning shots that skipped wildly on the water. King's boat had two seventy-horsepower outboard motors, and the *Honga River* dropped out of the chase after burning out a bearing in its engine. When Harvey King spotted the *McKeldin* bearing down on him, he pulled hard to port on the tiller, which brought him on a collision course with the *Honga River*. The officers on board the disabled boat continued to fire, and as King swerved the boat, Berkeley Muse yelled, "Oh! I've been hit!" and collapsed on the culling board. Another bullet struck King in the leg, and as the dredger struggled to get the motor boat to Reno Pier, Griffith held Muse's unconscious body. Griffith's hand was covered with blood and he could see that Muse was shot in the chest. The boat ran right up on the beach and Griffith yelled for the rescue squad. Before the ambulance arrived, Berkeley Muse lay dead in the boat.

The death of Berkeley Muse in a blaze of gunfire at dawn came just at the time Virginia and Maryland were creating a permanent bistate commission to bring peace to the troubled Potomac. At this time very few men were dredging oysters at Colonial Beach, and in the words of Calvin Dickinson, "To deliberately shoot a man in 1959 for taking oysters was going too far." Harvey King and his men had been unarmed, and the boat had gotten caught in a storm of bullets that was totally unnecessary. The town of Colonial Beach was shocked by Muse's tragic death, and the Maryland oyster police were warned to stay away from the Virginia shore. "Berkeley didn't need the money," said Landon Curley. "His family had plenty. He just loved to drudge oysters. Muse would have rather drudged oysters than go on vacation." Besides, added

Calvin Dickinson, "Drudgin' oysters wasn't the big thing that the Maryland police made it out." Three young men who got a thrill out of challenging the oyster police went out on the river that night, and Berkeley Muse did not return alive. "That was a sad time," reflected Landon Curley. When the police shot Berkeley Muse, the watermen of Colonial Beach knew that they were aiming to kill Virginians, not just disable their engines.

Muse's death precipitated a wide-ranging shake-up of the Maryland oyster police. While Howard Shenton urged the attorney general to use every legal device to prevent Officers Braun and Cooke from being brought to trial, he did initiate reforms that would be carried on by his successors. Henceforth the Tidewater Fisheries Commission trained its men better and made each officer take eighteen weeks of training with the Maryland State Police in community relations, the investigation of crimes, and the responsibility of firearms. Also, the oyster police ceased to be a political sinecure; applicants after 1959 were chosen on the basis of rigorous aptitude tests and examinations. In Captain Ellsworth Hoffman's words, "A marine police officer who acted the way they did on the Potomac in the 1950s wouldn't last a week on today's force."

In the months that followed Virginia and Maryland tried to settle their differences in order to avoid further bloodshed on the river. Negotiations hit a snag when the Maryland General Assembly refused to approve the new agreement after Virginia had already given its consent. Obstructionists in the state senate like Walter Dorsey of St. Mary's County and John Sanford of Worcester County didn't want control of the Potomac placed in the hands of a six-man bistate commission. Sanford and Dorsey believed that the new agreement would not pass a state-wide referendum, and they labored to put the issue on the ballot. Much to their surprise, the measure passed in the November elections and was forwarded to Washington for Congressional ratification. President John F. Kennedy signed the Potomac River Fisheries

Commission bill into law on December 5, 1962; the new law mandated the organization to conduct marine research as well as engage in seafood inspection. On that day Governor J. Millard Tawes and Governor Albertis S. Harrison of Virginia met at a festive luncheon on Capitol Hill to celebrate the end of generations of conflict and to inaugurate a new era of cooperation and conservation in the seafood industry between the two states. Oysters were the featured menu item.

The Potomac River war came to an end on that day, and since then no one has died in the Chesapeake Bay country over oysters. "We have other problems on the water now," says Captain Hoffman, "like narcotics, boaters in distress, and crimes usually associated with land activities. Oyster inspection has become a routine matter." Few people remember gunfire on the Chesapeake, and only a few oldtimers are left who can recall the days when a thousand sailing vessels worked on Tangier Sound and it seemed the oyster bonanza would never end.

Today tourists swarm to old oyster ports like Tilghman Island and St. Michaels and call these communities "picturesque" without bothering to investigate the region's history or understand its people. Looking back over forty years of life and work on Tangier Sound, Walt James of Deal's Island reflects that life on yesterday's Chesapeake "seems like a dream." When James started out in the 1930s, oyster sailing craft and steamboats abounded on Bay waters. The great boats have disappeared and, he laments, the Bay has little appeal these days. "That feeling of remoteness one experienced in the tidewater communities is no more. I am glad I knew it before the modern age took over." Each year men leave their skipjacks to rot in the marsh, and proud craft like the *Robert L. Webster* are purchased by preservation groups and affluent mariners for pleasure cruises and cocktail parties.

In the future those interested in the oyster wars of the Chesapeake Bay region will learn about them through books, local folklore, and yellowed newspaper accounts; and they will find that the saga of the oyster wars abounds in stories of courage, creative energy, and resourcefulness. It is of such things that noble visions and great lives, destined to resist the erosion of time and circumstance, are made.

Epilogue

THE VANISHING OYSTERMEN

IN TEN OR FIFTEEN YEARS the oystermen of Chesapeake Bay will be extinct, and their unique maritime culture and independent way of living will pass into folklore and history, much like that of the whaling men of New England. These Chesapeake men, who have pursued the oyster from the bottoms of the Bay for three centuries, have fallen victim to diminishing harvests, pollution, political indifference, and bureaucratic harassment.

No one can withstand the onslaught of economic realities. Oyster harvests have dropped in Chesapeake Bay from 125 million pounds of meat in 1880 to 25 million in 1978. According to Dr. George Krantz, a Bay scientist at the Horne's Point Environmental Laboratory in Cambridge, Maryland, poor oyster harvests are the result of poor spat-falls. The Chesapeake oysters are spawning, but the spat, or larvae, are not setting. Heavy amounts of fresh water pouring into the Bay, changing water temperatures, and pollution have a harmful impact on oysters in their nautilus stage when they are seeking to fix themselves to the sea bottom. Although Krantz believes that it may take ten or twenty years before it can be determined what is causing the spat not to set, one fact is obvious: "Man is the catalyst in bringing the oysters closer to extinction."

Chesapeake watermen don't have to be scientists to understand Bay research. It spells diminished income and a precarious and more competitive life as oystermen scramble for an increasingly scarce resource. Horne's Point scientists report that spat sets are running nearly 72 percent below

1968 figures, indicating a long-range crisis. Bob Ulanowicz, a biologist who uses a mathematical model to estimate oyster resources on his computer, calculates that the future oyster harvest will fall to 1.6 million bushels annually. Thus far his predictions have been remarkably accurate. In addition to the decline in natural spat sets, the Maryland Department of Natural Resources has curtailed its seed oyster planting operations. Oyster hatcheries are expensive, and, confronted with a budget-conscious legislature, the DNR has found that Bay conservation doesn't have a high financial priority.

Each year fewer men choose to follow the water. Out of 4,729 oystermen who applied to Annapolis for licenses in the 1978-1979 season, only about 1,500 were engaged full time in the business. Of the much-publicized skipjacks, that flotilla of sailing oyster dredges that numbered nearly a thousand at the turn of the century, only thirty-one worked the 1978-1979 season. Regardless of technique—dredging, hydraulic tonging, hand tonging, or more recently, scuba diving—oystering is becoming a part-time business on Chesapeake Bay.

No one has felt the changes in the industry more acutely than Pete Switzer, the dean of Tilghman's Island skipjack captains. Several years ago Captain Switzer was able to dredge his daily quota of 150 bushels in two hours. Now he is lucky to get 100 bushels after ten hours on the water. When the weather is bad or the Bay clogged with winter ice, Switzer may be held in port for weeks without income. After deducting expenses for his boat, the *Hilda Willing*, and pay for the crew, Switzer said that he made ten thousand dollars for the 1978-1979 season. It's far easier, he complains, to go into some other line of work. The skipjacks that still work the Bay are beginning to get waterlogged, and a new dredge boat costs seventy-five thousand dollars. Like other skipjack captains, Switzer will use his boat more in the future for the profitable summer tourist business.

Visitors to the Chesapeake region tend to romanticize the watermen and glorify their lifestyle. "Ain't no glory in oysterin'," reflected Milton Evans of Smith Island. "A man who doesn't want to work hard isn't going to make it in the water business." The Bay takes its toll. The men age quickly and are plagued by hernias, injuries, heart problems, and rheumatism. The Chesapeake is also dangerous. Many oystermen have lost their footing on the slippery planks of their boats and drowned. Boats are often lost in the rough waves churned up by unexpected storms. In the spring of 1977, Captain Thompson Wallace, a black waterman from Deal's Island, and his brother, son, and nephew were drowned when their boat, the *Claude Somers*, foundered in heavy seas. Folklorists may glamorize life in the Bay country, but oystermen have no illusions about the mighty Chesapeake. Thus watermen tend to be fatalists and inveterate gamblers. They have been known to lose hundreds of dollars in poker games and shuffleboard in local taverns; and many a Chesapeake woman knows the turbulent lifestyle that comes from being married to a "Hell-raisin' hard luck waterman."

The oystermen of the Chesapeake see the Department of Natural Resources as the chief villain in their struggles. According to Larry Simms, president of the three thousand-member Maryland Watermen's Association, the DNR is the tool of sport-fishing and recreational-boating interests and "the big money men who want to lease up the Bay bottom as they have done in other states." An oysterman who is trying to make a living on the Bay, Simms states, "has to come up against the DNR's dictatorial bureaucracy." The DNR, he explains, harasses, taxes, regulates, and supervises oystermen right out of business. "They treat us watermen as a nuisance and would like to get rid of us."

Although Maryland watermen usually produce 30 percent of the nation's oyster catch each year, they are politically weak. Highly individualistic, they feud among themselves on a host of issues and lack the numbers or the discipline necessary to win the support of the legislature on economic issues affecting watermen. Compared to other Chesapeake interests, the chemical companies, bayside developers, electric utilities, and sports-fishing groups, oystermen simply don't have the political clout.

The vanishing skipjack. Photograph: Orlando Wootten.

The vanishing watermen. Photograph: Orlando Wootten.

THE VANISHING OYSTERMEN

The worst enemy, and the most invidious, is pollution. It is hard to fix blame and even harder to generate popular support when Bay pollution arises from so many sources and jurisdictions. According to the Johns Hopkins Chesapeake Bay Institute, about 400 million gallons of sewage effluent are pumped into the Bay every day; scientists are hard pressed to tell whether the sewage or the chlorine used to treat it is more dangerous to the oysters and Bay wildlife. From industrial plants and farms come mercury, kepone, cadmium, pesticides, and herbicides. Vast amounts of phosphates and nitrates also flow into the Bay, accelerating the growth of algae and preventing sunlight from reaching underwater plants that are the beginning of the Chesapeake food chain.

Of the pollutants, oystermen fear oil the most. As the majority of Chesapeake commerce consists of oil tankers, watermen are apprehensive that a few major oil spills will wipe out the oyster beds. Studies conducted by the Virginia Institute of Marine Science have shown that oysters will not strike in areas contaminated by oil spills. At the moment, this problem is particularly acute in the Virginia side of the Chesapeake. After a bitter three-year fight, watermen and conservationists lost the battle to prevent the Hampton Roads Energy Corporation from building an oil refinery on the Elizabeth River near Portsmouth. Although the high cost of oil has prompted the company to use coal, John De Maria, president of the Virginia Watermen's Association, still worries that if an oil refinery is built, it will be "just down from the world's largest oyster producing area—the James River. An oil spill there would wipe out the seed oysters for the entire state of Virginia." The wreck of one large sixty-million-gallon oil tanker anywhere in Chesapeake Bay would probably eliminate most of the estuary's marine resources.

The lack of coordination of Bay affairs between Washington, Annapolis, and Richmond further exacerbates the problems of the Chesapeake and its oystermen. Until recently, federal-state relations in the region were characterized by bureaucratic confusion, duplicated programs, and misguided legislation based on economic self-interest. In 1978 Virginia and Maryland formed the Chesapeake Bay Legislative Advisory Commission to manage the Bay as a common resource. At this point it is too early to ascertain whether the "Chesapeake Circus" of politicians, scientists, environmentalists, and watermen will form an effective coalition to govern the Bay wisely.

Larry Simms worries that such advisory commissions will turn on the oystermen. It is much easier, he notes, to regulate the oystermen than to control pollution in the Bay. If oyster harvests are diminishing, then the easiest thing to do is to reorganize the industry: in effect, put the watermen out of business.

Oystering as it now exists is an inefficient business. As Varley Lang, a veteran waterman puts it, "Oystering is the one trade in the country in which efficiency is to be shunned and deplored. On the whole, the less efficiency in the tools for taking oysters, the better for all concerned." Using a technology that has changed little in three hundred years, oystermen roam the Chesapeake and treat it as a common resource to be exploited. "If a waterman caught the last oyster in Chesapeake Bay," quips Lionel Bennet of Crisfield, "he'd sell it." Watermen argue that the DNR should give them sufficient economic assistance so that they can continue working in the traditional manner.

Bay scientists and the DNR view the matter differently. Dr. George Krantz and other marine biologists have urged the watermen to begin "oyster farming" on leased Chesapeake bottom. Scientists have found that leased beds which are planted and cultivated like a farm crop could increase yields from eleven bushels per marine acre to twenty-five bushels. The oyster farms would be stocked with seed oysters spawned in hatcheries. Rebuilding the Chesapeake oyster harvests, the DNR and biologists concede, will require major changes in the industry. With new management of the Bay resources will come the end of the commons and the advent of scientifically managed, leased oyster bars—all antithetical to the oysterman's way of life. "What they want," lament the oystermen, "is to have us punching time clocks on the Chesapeake." While there will always be oysters, there soon won't be watermen to hunt them. The oystermen of the Bay country are being overwhelmed by the problems of an urban technological society; and their passing will scarcely be noticed.

Appendix I

THE MARYLAND OYSTER NAVY—1891

JOSEPH B. SETH,
COMMANDER

Vessel	Captain
Steamships	
Governor McLane	Thomas C. B. Howard
Governor Thomas	James Turner
Schooners	
Julia Hamilton	Samuel Tyler
Frolic	A. S. Bryan
Helen M. Baughman	Joseph H. Horney
Nellie Jackson	George Insley
Sloops	
Bessie Woolford	Joshua H. Thomas
Katie Hines	Thomas H. Ching
Eliza Hayward	Thomas F. Bridges
E. B. Groome	Charles W. Frazier
Carrie Franklin	I. F. Insley
Louisa Whyte	L. C. Cook

Source: Baltimore *Sun*, August 25, 1891.

Appendix II

OUTPUT OF MARYLAND OYSTERS,
1839-1910 (in bushels)

Year	Amount
1839	710,000
1850	1,350,000
1856	2,610,000
1858	3,500,000
1865	4,879,000
1869	9,233,000
1874	14,000,000
1884	15,000,000
1889	9,945,000
1897	7,254,000
1904	4,500,000
1910	3,500,000

Source: Caswell Grave, *History of the Oyster in Maryland*, (Baltimore: 1912).

BIBLIOGRAPHY

MANUSCRIPTS AND DISSERTATIONS

Oyster Seller's Account Book, Ms 835, Maryland Historical Society.

Thomas Ewell Scrapbook of the Oyster Conflict, Ms 351, Maryland Historical Society.

U.S. Supreme Court Library, Case # 1054, *Wharton v. Wise*, April 23, 1894.

Louis N. Whealton, "The Maryland and Virginia Boundary Controversy, 1668–1894" (PhD dissertation, Johns Hopkins University, 1897).

MARYLAND STATE DOCUMENTS

G. F. Beaven, *Maryland's Oyster Problem* (Solomon's Island: May 1945).

Commissioner of Labor and Statistics, *31st Annual Report, 1922* (Baltimore: 1923).

Hunter Davidson, *Report upon the Oyster Resources of Maryland* (Annapolis: 1870).

———, *Report on the Fisheries and Waterfowl of Maryland* (Annapolis: 1872).

Disbursements of the State Fishery Force (Annapolis: 1885).

Fish and Oyster Laws of the State of Maryland (Annapolis: 1913).

William J. Kennedy, *Report on State Fisheries to Governor Edwin Warfield* (Annapolis: October 29, 1906).

Maryland, *Shellfish Commission Report, 1907* (Annapolis: 1908).

BIBLIOGRAPHY

————, *Shellfish Commission Report, 1909* (Annapolis: 1910).

————, *Shellfish Commission Report, 1913* (Annapolis: 1914).

————, *Shellfish Commission Report, 1914-1915* (Annapolis: 1916).

A. J. Nichol, *The Oyster Packing Industry of Baltimore: Its History and Current Problems* (Baltimore: 1937).

Public Local Laws of Maryland, Vol. 2 (Baltimore: 1888).

Potomac River Oyster Pollution Commission Report (Washington, D.C.: 1912).

Records of Licenses Issued to Take Oysters in the State of Maryland and Several Counties (Annapolis: 1893).

Report of the Oyster Commission of the State of Maryland (Annapolis: 1884).

Report of the Board of Shellfish Commissioners (Annapolis: 1907).

"St. Michaels Oyster Report" 1895, Box 11, Hall of Records, Maryland State Publications.

William E. Timmons, *Report on the Oyster Fisheries of Maryland* (Annapolis: 1874).

R. V. Truitt, *Aspects of the Oyster Season in Maryland* (Annapolis: 1927).

JOURNALS, MAGAZINES, AND NEWSPAPERS

"American Oyster Culture," *Scribner's Magazine,* December 1877.

"The Battle of Chester River," *Frank Leslie's Illustrated Newspaper,* April 19, 1881.

Pearl Blood, "Oystering in the Chesapeake," *Journal of Geography,* January 1939.

"Battle of the Choptank," Baltimore *Sun,* June 14, 1889.

"Chesapeake Oyster Beds," *New York Times,* August 31, 1883.

"The Chesapeake Oyster Industry," *Harper's,* September 30, 1893.

BIBLIOGRAPHY

"Dredgers Come Off Victors," Baltimore *Sun*, January 14, 1889.

James W. England, "A Survey of the Oyster Industry," *Eastern Shore Magazine*, November 1937.

D. B. Fitzgerald, "With the Oyster Police," *Lippincott's Magazine*, January 1888.

John Kobler, "They've Been Fighting 173 Years," *Saturday Evening Post*, November 1, 1958.

Aubrey Land, "Economic Base and Social Structure: The 18th Century Chesapeake," *Journal of Economic History*, Vol. 25, 1965.

Ivy B. McNamara, "I Remember Dredging Oysters Through Ice," Baltimore *Sun*, December 26, 1954.

"The Maryland Oyster Business," *Harper's*, March 2, 1889.

"Oyster Export Trade," *New York Times*, February 19, 1878.

"A Peninsular Canaan," *Harper's Monthly Magazine*, May 1879.

"Poached Oysters," *Harper's*, March 4, 1884.

Garret Power, "More About Oysters Than You Wanted to Know," *Maryland Law Review*, Vol. 30, Summer 1970.

Lorie C. Quinn, "The Chesapeake Bay Country," *Crisfield Times*, January 14, 1944.

J. Richardson, "American Oyster Culture," *Scribner's Magazine*, December 1877.

Ralph J. Robinson, "Life Aboard the Oyster Dredges—1880," Baltimore *Sunday Sun Magazine*, November 24, 1952.

Samuel T. Sewell, "I Remember Oyster Dredging in the 1890s," Baltimore *Sunday Sun*, March 6, 1966.

"Steam Dredging Oysters," *New York Times*, December 9, 1879.

Bayard Taylor, "Down on the Eastern Shore," *Harper's Monthly Magazine*, September 1871.

George Alfred Townsend, "The Chesapeake Peninsula," *Scribner's Magazine*, March 1872.

BIBLIOGRAPHY

John R. Wennersten, "The Almighty Oyster: A Saga of Old Somerset and the Eastern Shore, 1850–1920," *Maryland Historical Magazine*, March 1979.

Edward L. Wilson, "The Biography of the Oyster," *Scribner's Magazine*, January 1891.

Robert Wilson, "On the Eastern Shore," *Lippincott's Magazine*, August 1876.

————, "The Peninsula," *Lippincott's Magazine*, July 1876.

Woodrow T. Wilson, "Crisfield in 1878," *Crisfield Times*, March 20, 1970.

Orlando Wootten, "The Glory of Yesterday's Deal Island," *Salisbury Times*, January 13, 1974.

BOOKS AND PAMPHLETS

W. N. Armstrong, *Notes on the Oyster Industries of Virginia*. Hampton, Va, 1879.

Charles A. Barker, *The Background of the Revolution in Maryland*. New Haven, 1940.

Robert and George Barrie, *Cruises, Mainly in the Bay of the Chesapeake*. Philadelphia, 1909.

Hector Bolitho, *The Glorious Oyster*. New York, 1961.

Wendell P. Bradley, *They Live By the Wind*. New York, 1968.

M. V. Brewington, *Chesapeake Bay: A Pictorial Maritime History*. Cambridge, Md., 1953.

————, *Chesapeake Bay Log Canoes and Bugeyes*. Cambridge, Md., 1963.

Carl Bridenbaugh, *Myths and Realities: Societies of the Colonial South*. Baton Rouge, 1963.

William K. Brooks, *The Oyster: A Popular Summary of a Scientific Study*. Baltimore, 1891.

Robert Burgess, *This Was Chesapeake Bay*. Cambridge, Md., 1963.

Hulbert Footner, *Maryland Main and the Eastern Shore*. New York, 1942.

BIBLIOGRAPHY

————, *Rivers of the Eastern Shore*. New York, 1944.

Caswell Grave, *A History of the Oyster in Maryland*. Annapolis, 1912.

John and Karen Hess, *The Taste of America*. New York, 1977.

Meredith Janvier, *Baltimore in the Eighties and Nineties*. Baltimore, 1933.

Varley Lang, *Follow the Water*. Winston-Salem, 1961.

Arthur P. Middleton, *Tobacco Coast: A Maritime History of Chesapeake Bay in the Colonial Era*. Newport News, 1953.

James Murray, *History of Pocomoke City*. Baltimore, 1883.

Hamilton Owens, *Baltimore on the Chesapeake*. Garden City, 1941.

Joseph B. Seth, *Recollections of a Long Life on the Eastern Shore*. Easton, Md., 1926.

Arthur Sherwood, *Understanding the Chesapeake*. Cambridge, Md., 1973.

William I. Tawes, *God, Man, Saltwater, and the Eastern Shore*. Cambridge, Md., 1977.

R. W. Todd, *Methodism of the Peninsula*. Philadelphia, 1886.

Edward Noble Vallandigham, *Delaware and the Eastern Shore*. Philadelphia, 1922.

Adam Wallace, *Parson of the Islands*. Cambridge, Md., 1961.

Woodrow T. Wilson, *History of Crisfield and Surrounding Areas of Maryland's Eastern Shore*. Baltimore, 1973.

Charles M. Yonge, *Oysters*. London, 1960.

INDEX

Accomac County, Virginia, 94
Acree, David, 112-13
Amanda F. Lewis, 99
American Revolution, 8, 9
Annapolis, 50, 51, 61, 77, 78, 79, 84, 97, 101, 108, 114
Annemessex River, 41, 48, 86
Atwell, Wilson, Bozo, 117-19
Avalon, police sloop, 41

Baltimore, 13, 14, 28, 56, 70
Baltimore and Ohio Railroad, 14
Baltimore Clipper Ships, 14
Baltimore Hibernian Society, 61
Baltimore Maritime Hospital, 55
Bennet, Lionel, 134
Bessie Jones, 92, 93
Bessie Woolford, 45, 136
Biddleman, Edward, 62, 63
Blackstone Island, 101
Black watermen, 23, 25, 35, 56, 63, 64, 65, 72, 73, 83, 130
Blizzard, John, 18
Bohanan, C.M., 92
Boye, Fritz, 59
Bradshaw, Haynie, 18-20
Branford, John, 99
Breton Bay, 93
Brewington, M.V., 99
Brice, Arthur, 115
Bridges, Thomas F., 136
Brooks, William K., 89; *The Oyster: A Popular Summary of a Scientific Study*, 88
Brown, George, Governor, 62

Bryan, A.S., 136
Bucheimer, Fred, 74
Bugeyes, 99
Burgess, John, 18
Burgess, Robert, 99

Callister, Henry, 8
Calvert, Philip, 46
Cambridge, Md., 22, 23, 76, 83, 84
Camp meetings, 10, 21
Cape Henry, Va., 6
Carmon, John Lee, 27
Carrie Franklin, 36
Carrie Stevens, 23
Castus, James, 83
Cator, Charles B., 83
Charles County, 102
Chesapeake Bay, 5
  Legislative Advisory Commission, 134
Chesapeake Zoological Laboratory, 88
Chester River, 9, 30, 36, 41, 72, 73, 74, 77, 79, 82, 84
Chestertown, Md., 6, 41, 72, 74, 78
Ching, Thomas H., 136
Choptank River, 9, 22, 30, 36, 38, 52, 102
City of Norfolk, 22
Civil War, 11, 14
Claude Somers, 130
Clements, James, 39-42
Clows, "China," 9
Cobb Oyster Bar, 92
Colonial Beach, Va., 106, 108, 109, 117, 120, 124, 125

143

INDEX

Connel Oyster Bar, 98
Conrad, Julius, 61
Consumers Ice Company, 100
Cook, L.C., 136
Cooper, Frank, 63-68
Corsica incident, 79, 84
Coulbourn, Isaac, 27
Courtney, Arthur, 64, 66, 67
Cox, Ernest, 98
Creighton, Amos, 114
Crisfield, John W., 16, 17
Crisfield, Md., 17, 18, 21, 26, 47, 48,
    70, 71, 76, 100
Crockett, Riggin, and Company, 71
Crowder, Oliver, 79, 80
Cullison, Chester, 109, 111, 115,
    119; Curley, Landon, 107-9,
    116-19, 124

Dahlgren Artillery Range, 107
Davidson, Hunter, 37, 38, 41, 42,
    43, 49, 50, 74; *Report Upon
    the Oyster Resources of
    Maryland*, 49
Davis, Joseph, 115
Deal's Island, 9, 10, 11, 64
DeBroca, Paul, 52
DeMaria, John, 133
Dickinson, Calvin, 121, 124
Dorchester County, 23, 52, 62, 83,
    84, 96, 101
    Oyster Militia, 84
Dorsey, Walter, 125
Dryden, L.T., 48

Earle, Swepson, 90
Eastern Bay, 37
Easton, Md., 76
E.B. Groome, 83, 136
Eliza Hayward, 82, 136
Ella Agnes, 56
Ella F. Cripps, 93
Eva, 59, 60
Evans, George, 85
Evans, Milton, 130
Evans, Stewart H., 63
Evans, William, 71
Ewell, Thomas J., 66, 67

Field, Abiathar, 14
Field, George, 21
Florence, 27, 73
Frazier, Charles W., 83, 136
Frolic, 136

George, William T., 74, 77, 78
Gibson, William, 71
Goldsborough, Philip, Governor,
    101
Goodsell, J.H., 27
Governor McLane, 63, 79, 80, 82,
    84, 86, 96, 136
Governor Thomas, 82, 86, 96, 136
Great Rocks Oyster Bar, 45, 48
Griffith, John, 123

Haase, Ferdinand, 59
Haman Act, 97, 98
Haman, B. Howard, 97
Hampton Roads Energy Corpora-
    tion, 133
Hand windlass, tyranny of, 63
Harris, Alex, 93
Harrison, Albertis S., Governor of
    Virginia, 126
Helen M. Baughman, 78, 136
Henninghausen, Louis P., 61
Hilda Willing, 129
Himan, George, 86
Hoffman, Ellsworth, 113, 125, 126
Hog Island dispute, 85, 86
Honga River, 43
Honga River, 121, 123, 124
Hoopers Island, 62
Hoopers Straits, 43
Horne's Point Environmental Lab-
    oratory, 128
Horney, Joseph H., 136
Howard, Thomas, C.B., 80, 82, 136
Hurricane of 1933, 103, 104

Ida Augusta, 84, 85, 86
Insley, George, 136
Insley, I.F., 136
Involuntary servitude, 55, 56, 62,
    63
Irvington, Va., 64

INDEX

Jackson, Elihu, Governor, 84, 86
James River, Va., 95, 133
James V. Daiger, 64
James, Walt, 126
J.C. Mahoney, 42, 76, 78, 80
Jenkins, Charles K., 92
Johns Hopkins University, 88
Johnson, Harvey, 21
Joppa, 66, 67
Julia Hamilton, 136
Jullia H. Jones, 80

Katie Hines, 136
Kellam, Alex, 103, 104
Kennedy, John F., President, 125
Kent, 104
Kent County, 38, 50, 72, 73, 78, 96
Kent Island, 6
King, Harvey, 119-124
Kite, 74, 78
Krantz, George, 128, 134

Landon, Viola, 101
Lang, Varley, 134
Langrall, James, 52
Lankford, William, 59, 60
Lawson, 85
Lawson, Henry, 85
Lawson, Isaac, 48
Leila, 37, 42, 43, 51, 52
Lewis, Charles R., 84, 85
Long, Coulbourn and Company, 72
Louisa Whyte, 136
Little Choptank River, 82, 83
Little Craig, 117, 118
Log canoes, 11
Long Island Sound, N.Y., 68

McCready, Robert H., 41
McKeldin, 124
McKeldin, Theodore, Governor,
    115, 119, 121
McNamara, Ivy B., 102
Maddell, James F., 77
Maddox, George, 92
Major Murrey, 98
Makemie, Francis, 6
Maltby, Caleb S., 13, 16

Maltby House Hotel, 13
Mann, William Hodges, Governor
    of Virginia, 101
Manokin River, 43, 73, 98
Marshall, John, 84
Marine Police, *See* Maryland Oys-
    ter Navy
Martin, Luther, 9
Mary Compton, 39, 41
Maryland
    Colonization Society, 23
    Conservation Commission, 111
    Department of Natural Re-
        sources, 129, 130, 134, 135
    Fisheries Commission, 101
    General Assembly, 51, 61
    German Society, 58, 61, 62
    Oyster Commission, 88, 98
    Oyster Navy, 37, 39, 41, 42, 43,
        45, 48, 50, 51, 70, 73,
        74, 79, 82, 84, 86, 89, 92, 95,
        96, 102, 104, 107, 109, 112,
        113, 115, 117, 119, 121, 125,
        136
    Shell Fish Commission, 98, 101
    Tidewater Fisheries Commis-
        ion, 108, 109, 112, 113, 114,
        117, 118, 119, 121, 123, 125
    Watermen's Association, 130
Maryland-Virginia marine bound-
    ary disputes, 46, 47, 84, 85,
    87, 94, 108, 109, 113, 114,
    116, 119, 124, 125; Jenkins-
    Black Award of 1877, 48; Mc-
    Cready v. *Virginia* (1876), 94;
    Potomac River Compact of
    1785, 47, 92, 94, 112, 114,
    121, 122; Potomac River oys-
    ter tax controversy, 116;
    Wharton v. *Wise* (1894), 94
Mayher, Otto, 58-60, 68
Merrick, 74
Methodism, 9, 10, 11
Methodist, 10
Miles River, 9, 38, 42
Millstone Landing, 92
Miss Ann, 119, 120
Monroe Creek, Va., 107, 116

INDEX

Mosquito Fleet, 108
Muir, Sylvester, 100
Muse, Berkeley, 122-25

Nannie Merryman, 74
Nanticoke Indians, 5
Nanticoke River, 73
Negroes, *See* Black watermen
Nellie Jackson, 136
Nelson, Christopher, 27
Nelson, Earl, 113
Nelson, Tull, and Company, 72
Newtown Manor, 92
Noble, Thomas, 117-19

Olive, 25, 32
Onancock, Virginia, 84, 85, 94
Oyster, 96
Oyster culture, history of, 3-4
Oyster industry (Maryland), Baltimore, 63, 69; conservation, 88, 95, 96, 97; Crisfield, 71; culling law, 69, 89; decline of, 53, 87, 100, 104, 128; dredging, 30, 35; employment in, 89; leased oyster beds, 97, 101, 130; licensing, 96, 129; output of industry (1839-1910), 137; oyster farming, 99, 134, 135; oyster inspectors, 90; pollution, 90, 95, 101, 128, 133; seed oysters, 95; spat sets, measurement of, 129; "tragedy of the commons," 95
Oyster pirates, 74, 77, 78, 80, 82, 83, 115
Oyster resources, Virginia, 6, 7, 84, 133
Oxford, Md., 6, 23, 25, 26, 76

Partnership, 63
Paddies, 55, 58
Page, Henry, 67
Phillips, Milford, 89
Phoebus Harry, 115
Pocomoke, 109
Pocomoke City, Md., 72

Pocomoke River, 47, 94
Pocomoke Sound, 47, 48, 90, 93, 94
Port Tobacco Creek, 98
Potomac River, 5, 46, 47, 63, 72, 82, 84-87, 90, 92, 93, 96, 101, 102, 108, 109, 111, 117, 119, 121
Potomac River
   Fisheries Commission, 125
   Oyster Pollution Commission, 101
Power, Garret, 98
Princess Anne, Md., 67, 98
Prohibition, 102
Pungies, 99

Queen Anne's County, 78
Quinn, Lorie, 62

Raisin, Isaac, 39, 50
Rea, Lynn, 56
Read, A.J., 49
Reed, Stanley, Justice, 122
Regulator, 52
Revelle, W.E., 90
Rice, Gus, 42, 43, 76, 77, 78, 80
Richardson, James, 28
Riggin, Severn, 20
Robert L. Webster, 100, 126
Rock Hall, Md., 43, 71
Rollins, Albert, 119
Rowe, H.C., 68, 69
Rowe and Company, 69
Roy, Dempsey, 119
Russel, Douglas, 92, 93
Russell, George R., 86
Russell, William F., 84, 85
Ryland, William, 116

St. Clement's Bay, 92
St. Mary's County, 92, 93, 96, 102, 108, 109
St. Michaels, Md., 25, 28, 32, 33, 42, 43, 71, 126
Salisbury, Md., 22
Salsette, 68
Samuel J. Pentz, 25
Sanford, John, 125

INDEX

Sayer, Louis, 93
Scarborough, Edmund, 47
Seth, Joseph B., 86, 96
Sewell, Samuel T., 35
Shakespeare Saloon, 21
Shanghaing Act of 1908, 63, *See also* Involuntary servitude
Shenton, Howard, 123, 125
Shores, Robert Lee, 114
Simms, Larry, 130, 134
Sinepuxent Bay, 95
Skipjacks, 100, 129
Smith Island, 18, 20, 48, 49, 84, 102, 103
Smith, John, Captain, 5, 6
Smith, Will, 103
Smith's Point, 47
Somers Cove, 16, *See also* Crisfield, Md.
Somers, Michael, 16
Somerset County, 43, 52, 59, 60, 73, 101
Stanley, Thomas, Governor of Virginia, 118
Sterling, J. and Company, 71
Stevens, John, 23
Swan Point, 38, 43
Swann Point Oyster Bar, 107
Switzer, Pete, 129
Sykes, Walter, 63

Talbot County, 33, 96
Tangier Island, Virginia, 9, 10
Tangier Sound, 9, 16, 30, 45, 46, 47, 48, 53, 62, 104, 126
Tawes, Isaac, 27
Tawes, J. Millard, Governor, 36, 126
Tawes James B., 100, 101
Tawes, John, 115-17
Taylor, Bayard, 16
Taylor, Henry, 64-67
T.B. Schall, 83
Thomas, Joshua, 10
Thomas, Joshua, Captain, 136
Thoreau, Henry David, 14
Tieck, Heinrich, 62, 63
Tilghman Island, 102, 126, 129

Timmons, William, 50
Tiny Lou, 119
Tred Avon River, 23
Tull, Frank, 66
Tull, James, 71, 72
Turner, James, 136
Tyler, Nola, 103
Tyler, Samuel, 136

Ulanowicz, Robert, 129
U.S.S. Ohio, 102

Venus, 81, 109
Viola, 63
Virginia
    Fisheries Commission, 112
    Institute of Marine Science, 133
    Oyster Militia, 49, 86, 116
    Watermen's Association, 133

Wallace, Adam, 9
Wallace, David, 113
Wallace, Thompson, 130
Warfield, Edward, 11
War of 1812, 10
Washington, George, 7, 47
Watermen, social life of, 32, 33, 35, 72, 98, 102, 104, 122, 130; *See also* Black watermen
Webster, Jacob Wesley, 45, 46
Westmoreland County, Va., 92, 106
Whaland, Joe, 8
Wharton, Robert, 94
Whitehaven, 72
Wicomico River, 8, 41, 43, 72, 73
Wilson, John, 72, 73, 74
Winslow, Francis, 51, 53, 88
Wise, Henry A., 48
Worcester County, 95
Wroten, T.E., 90
Wye River, 38
Wyman, Walter, 55

Yates, Charles C., 96; *Yates Survey of the Oyster Bars of Maryland*, 96, 97